£ 17.95

CW00746443

Financial Engineering:
The effective financial
management of business

by
Jorge Gabrielczyk, B.Sc(Eng), ACGI, FCA

London
Fourmat Publishing
1986

ISBN 1 85190 018 7

First published November 1986

With the exception of public limited companies, the
companies referred to in this book are entirely fictitious.

© 1986 J J Gabrielczyk
Published by Fourmat Publishing, 27 & 28 St Albans Place,
Islington Green, London N1 0NX
Printed in Great Britain by
Billing & Sons Limited, Worcester

Preface

Every enterprise in business to make a profit goes through a process of financial engineering. It does so to fix selling prices for new products, to quote for bulk orders, to evaluate the benefits of taking on new staff or of expansion of premises, or to negotiate for new capital.

Financial engineering is much more than an accountant's look at the financial consequences of a business decision. Financial engineering is the process of identifying and reducing uncertainty in the making of business decisions. Thus, it is an active aid to the effective management of the business as a whole.

This book has been written primarily for experienced business managers who need to know of financial techniques so as to improve their performance and that of the business which they own or for which they are responsible. It is assumed that the reader has minimal financial knowledge, and that such as may be possessed has been gained through the unstructured medium of experience.

For that reason, the book commences with a basic analysis of financial information in two Chapters. Chapter 1 reviews the type and quality of information which is available to help decision-making in business and the uses to which that information can be put. Chapter 2 provides a fundamental outline of the way in which information is captured, collected and interpreted.

Chapters 3 to 7 look inwards to the management of the business as a living entity. The capital structure of a business determines its exposure to risk and the costs it has to commit in order to service the providers of that capital. The advantages and disadvantages and costs of different types of funding are examined in detail. The split between fixed costs and variable costs determines the pace at which a business must work in order to pay for those fixed costs. The level of fixed asset investment will determine the degree of momentum to be overcome when implementing change. These Chapters contrast long and short-range assets and decisions. The different financial techniques available to assess each area are discussed and where appropriate, illustrated with examples.

The final part of the book deals with the way in which financial information can be used in connection with outsiders. Chapter 8 deals with the approach to the raising of funds. Chapter 9 considers how published accounts can be used to gain insights into the financial position of competitors, suppliers or customers. Chapter 10 takes the reader into the world of the Stock Exchange.

Taxation is largely outside the scope of this book. Although all business decisions have taxation implications, few are initiated purely for tax reasons. Instead, it is sound practice (and relatively straightforward) to take professional tax advice about a sound, well financially engineered business proposal. In the first instance, this book aims to help the reader construct that sound business proposal.

Many readers will find the first Chapters difficult, not because of any intrinsic difficulty, but because of the spate of new terms with which they may not be familiar. There is a comprehensive Glossary at the rear of the book which is designed to cope with this problem.

This book has grown out of the intensive financial training courses developed and conducted specifically for senior executives by the author. Many individuals have contributed to its development, but in particular, I would like to single out my friends (and subjects) at Holiday Inns and Marks & Spencer, who provided encouragement, enthusiasm and a ready and receptive testbed for new ideas.

JJG
September 1986

This book is dedicated to my wife, Maria, who served as a sounding board, and to my eight-month old daughter, Anne-Marie, who did her best to distract my attention away from writing.

Contents

		page
Chapter 1	**Using financial information**	1
	1. The purposes of information	3
	2. The users of financial information and their perspectives	11
	3. The purpose of profit	14
	4. The role of cash	15
	5. A financial engineer's information checklist	17
Chapter 2	**Accounting concepts and techniques**	22
	1. Business entities	22
	2. Principles of book-keeping	24
	3. Calculation of accounting profit	32
	4. The balance sheet	35
	5. The cash flow effects of accounting conventions	36
	6. Depreciation and amortisation	37
Chapter 3	**Sources of funds and cost of capital**	40
	1. The cost of capital	40
	2. Shareholders' risk	41
	3. Borrowing capacity	45
	4. Permanent capital	51
	5. Calculation of cost of capital	58
Chapter 4	**The business as a system of costs and revenues**	61
	1. The nature of costs and revenues	62
	2. Value added and contribution	67
	3. Breakeven	69
	4. Breakeven and pricing	76

Chapter 5 **Managing business assets: working capital**   89
    1. Working capital   91
    2. Management of stocks   96
    3. Management of debtors   102

Chapter 6 **Managing business assets: capital projects**   108
    1. Capital budgeting   109
    2. The appraisal process   110
    3. The impact of risk and uncertainty   125

Chapter 7 **Control and analysis of performance** 135
    1. Optimising long range performance   135
    2. Control of short term performance   139
    3. Ratio analysis of management accounts   146

Chapter 8 **The financing proposal**   154
    1. Assessing funding needs   155
    2. Deciding whom to approach   162
    3. Predicting and presenting the returns available   163

Chapter 9 **Published accounts**   166
    1. The objectives of published accounts   167
    2. The legislation   172
    3. The components of a set of published accounts   173
    4. Accounting conventions   176
    5. Analysing published accounts   181

Chapter 10 **Corporate finance**   187
    1. The Stock Exchange   187
    2. Finance for private companies   190
    3. Mergers and acquisitions   193
    4. Management buy-outs   194

Appendix 1 Statements of Standard Accounting Practice (SSAPs)   196

Appendix 2 Glossary   202

Index   211

Chapter 1

Using financial information

Information is the medium to which the financial engineer applies his tools. For that reason, he needs to be thoroughly conversant with the properties of that medium in exactly the same way as any engineer needs to be thoroughly conversant with the physical properties of the materials he works with. He must know what information he needs, where it can be obtained, its accuracy and its suitability for his purpose.

Information comes in many shapes and sizes, and from many sources. To some readers perhaps the most familiar examples of financial information are the annual accounts published by companies. To others, the internal management accounts produced by their own organisations are of great importance. Wherever capital is provided to an enterprise in exchange for a return which is to be produced by the skills of the managers of that enterprise, the success or failure of that business will ultimately be measured in terms of historical financial performance. Externally or internally, the prime indicator of this financial performance will take the form of financial accounting. In this way a reading of financial status by means of accounts can serve the same purpose as a reading taken from a voltmeter or a pressure gauge. Both try to report on what is going on.

However, accounts suffer from the same deficiencies as all other measuring instruments:

- the wrong information may be inadvertently read (operator error);

1

- the conventions which underlie the collection of data may not be understood;
- the presentation of the results may be incorrectly interpreted.

We will consider the interpretation of accounts and the accounting conventions which underlie the preparation of accounts in later Chapters in this book. In this Chapter, we will review the kinds of financial information which we need to have available to us and the purposes to which it may be put, so that we can subsequently validly use that information for the financial engineering process.

But before starting, it is as well to sound a few words of warning:

The danger of accepting labels

Labels are commonly-used terms such as profitability, cash generation or cash hunger, high gearing and rate of return. All of these terms are frequently used to refer to financial status and condition. Most managers think that they know the meaning of those financial descriptions.

In fact, without further elaboration, most of these descriptions are financially meaningless. For example, "a profitable project" may be one that yields no cash returns for an unacceptably long period of time, and conversely "high gearing", with the right level of profitability, may be perfectly acceptable. In a similar way, quoted "rates of return" may give rise to misunderstanding or ambiguity, since there is more than one way of defining rates of return.

Financial engineering seeks to identify and improve the relationships between key business activities, costs, revenues and funding levels. In this context, labels are superficial and usually inadequate. They should be investigated and expanded to provide a comprehensive description of what is planned and what the full financial consequences are likely to be.

The danger of believing accounts

Most large companies produce management information periodically, generally in the form of management accounts, and all limited liability companies are required by law to produce annual statutory accounts. These two different types of accounts are produced for different purposes. They contain financial information summarised and presented in very different ways. We will review these major differences later on in this Chapter; suffice it to say for now that they are used by different people for a variety of different purposes.

What is more, there is a tendency to forget that accounts contain information based on assumptions once made by somebody in the organisation. Those assumptions may be out of date, they may be completely inappropriate for anything out of the ordinary, and they may not have been designed to cater for an unusual and unforeseen combination of circumstances.

Once again, financial engineering seeks to identify and improve the relationships between key business activities, costs, revenues and funding. Existing management accounts should be regarded with suspicion since they may imply relationships which no longer exist, or they may incorporate assumptions which are not valid for the situation under review.

1. The purposes of information

Management information is as much a business resource as the factory premises, the production line or the sales force. It should be managed in the same way as production, marketing, quality or service standards. That is to say, it should provide what the market needs. In the case of management information, the market is internal. It is up to each and every manager to determine what is needed.

Appropriately designed management information systems can provide, to use a structural engineering or building analogy, a report on "site conditions" within the business. Financial engineering techniques (of which more later) can then be applied to create improvements.

Thus the manager should have available to him management information prepared on a basis which he understands and in such a format and at such a time that it helps him to plan and control his element of the business.

Planning and control are among the most important aspects of running a business. They are also fundamental to the process of financial engineering:

> *Planning* is the design stage of the financial engineering project, just as in any other engineering task. During this process, the manager (engineer) designs the shape of his business in times to come by setting business goals and objectives.
>
> *Control* is the equivalent of site supervision, during which the manager ensures that the design is being followed and that any variations which are found to be necessary as the project progresses are implemented.

Managerial tasks in the planning and control area can be sub-divided into three functional segments:

- choosing between alternatives or selecting a no action option;
- anticipating the future and reacting to it;
- reporting the results of operations and taking corrective measures.

In each area there is a fundamental requirement for the right kind of information, so that financial engineering techniques can be validly applied to improve the quality of decisions.

Choosing between alternatives

In this particular area, more often than not, management decision-making involves the balancing of current costs against future benefits for a number of alternative courses of action. Costs are usually ascertainable with some degree of precision, but future benefits are much more difficult to assess. In order to permit a reasoned judgement to be made, managers need to have available information which enables them to evaluate the consequences of each of the alternative courses of action.

The types of decision which fall under this general heading include:

- Accepting courses of action which generate a minimum required level of income.

For example, a well-known multinational retailer does not invest in retail sites unless the forecast rate of return on his investment is at least 17%.

- Selecting the best out of a set of mutually exclusive options.

  For example, a small British manufacturer of hospital consumables has an opportunity to supply a very substantial order. However, to meet the call-off schedule demanded by the customer, the company has to acquire extra manufacturing facilities. Thus it appears to be faced with the choice of turning down the order, or of accepting the order but making a substantial enforced investment.

In such cases detailed specific information about cost and revenue behaviour is needed in order to make the correct managerial decisions. For instance:

- Those costs which vary with the level of activity need to be separated and considered separately from those costs which are independent of the level of activity.

  Probably the most familiar example of a variable cost in the manufacturing industry is the raw material element of the cost of production. That cost most often varies directly in proportion to the level of production. However, there are other costs of manufacture, such as the rates for the factory, or administrative office overheads, which do not change with varying production throughput levels.

- The relationship between activity levels and costs needs to be known for those costs which vary depending on the level of activity.

  Continuing with the example of a company in the manufacturing industry, some variable costs, such as the cost of raw materials (as mentioned above), will rise in direct proportion to throughput. Other costs, such as labour, may increase in steps. Some costs may even drop on a per-unit basis, as quantity price breaks become operative, or if set-up wastage can be spread over larger production runs.

- Costs which are already committed need to be separated from additional or voluntary costs which have yet to be incurred.

  For example, leasing charges and annual rates bills

are committed costs, as are the costs of any goods in stock. An example of a voluntary cost may be the cost of a future advertising campaign which may or may not be incurred depending on the exercise of managerial judgement. Naturally, only voluntary costs can be avoided.

The behavioural nature of costs and revenues will be described in rather more detail in Chapter 4, and we will see how behavioural segregation of costs can lead to a simple financial model of a business. In turn, that model can be used as a fundamental part of managerial decision-making.

Anticipating the future

Some managers claim that it is of little value to plan ahead, since any forward views are bound to be wrong. In the author's opinion those individuals misunderstand the nature of planning. Planning is not about preparing a detailed forecast of sales, profit, cash, etc. for the next *n* years. The future is uncertain, and those forecasts are bound to be wrong. The more extended the forecast, the more likely it is to be wrong, and thus of little value.

Planning is about linking a business organisation's objectives with its operating skills and constraints and the opportunities and threats which are presented to it. It is of necessity long-range in nature, since it involves identifying business areas and practices which need to be changed. The implementation of that change can be done successfully only over the longer term.

Objectives are in effect the design brief for the financial engineer. They may differ from business to business, but there is one particular business objective which is common to all commercial enterprises; that is the requirement for management to maximise return on the capital invested by the owners. No matter at what level within a commercial organisation managers may operate, they must view the application of financial engineering in the context of that particular business objective.

Operating skills and constraints must be known to the

financial engineer. Information about how the organisation responds to business stimuli (such as volume or price changes), and about factors which limit performance (such as capacity constraints) must be explicitly available.

Opportunities and threats are largely rooted in the economic environment external to the business, and in the main are outside the control of the business entity. Nevertheless, the financial engineer should have a knowledge of trends as they affect his business. For example, in the United Kingdom the current government-imposed reduction of the profits of pharmaceutical companies had its roots in a report commissioned in the mid-1960s, and the trend to strict control of prices (and advertising spend) was easily discernible in 1980 and earlier. Yet the industry did little to head off this threat until 1985, at which time it started a campaign to improve its public image. That campaign showed all the symptoms of too little, too late.

Thus effective planning requires knowledge of all the information already outlined in the previous section about choosing between alternatives. It also requires knowledge of trends in the economic environment in which the business functions, as well as information about the strengths and weaknesses of the business, of the factors which significantly influence performance, and of those aspects of the business which act as limiters or restrict performance.

These factors have to be completely integrated in order to take the business forward in an orderly and cohesive fashion. This process and the accompanying selection of business direction and strategy are generally termed corporate strategic planning.

Corporate planning and strategy is a subject in its own right, and many excellent and lengthy books have been written about it. A later Chapter of this book (Chapter 7) provides a summary, and an overview of the subject for the reader. For purposes of this introduction to financial engineering, we will assume that our brief has already been set in terms of business objectives, and that our task is to recommend action.

Under this heading, the types of decision which financial engineers might be asked to advise on include:

- Refinement or termination of a business activity.

  For example, of three factories, one is making a loss. Should it be closed? In fact this kind of question is an excellent example of the danger of using labels, and of believing accounts. The financial engineer should not respond until he knows precisely how the supposed loss is calculated (eg, before or after allocation of central administrative overheads — see also Chapter 4).

- Identification of factors which limit business performance under given conditions.

  For instance, the small hospital consumable manufacturer described earlier had insufficient manufacturing capacity to meet the call-off schedule required by its customer. Rather than invest substantial sums of money to provide manufacturing facilities which might have been used for that specific order only, the company investigated its capacity constraint in great detail and realised that it could manufacture the order by some modest modifications to the call-off. The company offered the customer a small discount in return for those amendments, and thereby turned a production problem into a marketing advantage — a good example of the importance of detailed, relevant information.

- Acquisition of additional business facilities or entry into new markets.

  The financial engineer may be asked whether it is worth adding an extension to an hotel, buying a new machine or acquiring a whole company. Information may be very sparse, and very often there are no right answers. There is nothing wrong with framing the response in terms of operating targets. "The hotel extension is viable (ie provides the right rate of return to our providers of capital) if we can achieve 60% occupancy in the new extension at an average rate of £32.00." The financial engineering parameters are then set out. It is up to the operators to assess whether they can achieve them.

- General revisions and amendments to plans and budgets.

Life never runs smoothly or according to plan. The financial engineer will be asked to assess the impact of change. As a result he will have to amend his evaluation of the future and report the effect of those changes. Once again, a knowledge of cost structures is vital, as well as an information capture system which flags the need for revision.

In all of these diverse areas, the specific information which is needed to make the correct managerial recommendations or choices includes:

- avoidable/unavoidable costs need to be separated (as previously described);
- incremental costs and their relationships with planned activities need to be identified;
- the effect of economic trends on cost structures needs to be identified;
- lead times for implementing change need to be known, so that they can be reflected in planning horizons.

Reporting the results of operations and taking corrective measures

The purpose of reporting results is twofold:

Firstly, the reports indicate the "score", or the historical performance. Thus they serve as a record of the effectiveness of the stewardship exercised by the managers of a business on behalf of the actual owners of that business.

Secondly, the reports serve as indicators of corrective action. In this capacity they are more concerned with using the past as an indicator of the future than with the creation of a meticulous record of historical events.

Clearly, for management purposes, the latter of the two functions outlined is the more important.

Corrective action can only be taken if costs can be classified by origin and by managerial responsibility. Simultaneously, authority for action which is commensurate with the responsibilities delegated needs to be granted to the appropriate managerial levels. In this way, planning and control are inseparably linked to organisational structure.

In this area, the information needs of managers can be quite simply described. They need to know:

- what has happened;
- what the cause was;
- who should take corrective action.

Information for making decisions

The information needs of financial engineers relate primarily to internal performance and to external opportunities. In many cases, information is needed about the future; but no such information may be available. Therefore, the past is used as a guide to the future.

All of the characteristics of the information which we typically need may be portrayed in the form of an "information window":

	INTERNAL INFORMATION	EXTERNAL INFORMATION
PAST	internal results achieved — eg — costs/revenues — overheads — productivity	external results achieved — eg — market share — share price — recruiting
FUTURE	forecast of ability to react to future conditions	the likely future external stimuli

In summary, the information which is available for managerial decision-making varies in quality. Information about the future is at best a calculated guess, and at worst just a guess. Information about the past should be quite reliable, providing it is free of misleading labels and properly stratified by behavioural characteristics.

It is worth presenting diagrammatically these differences in quality of information, since we will use this grading to make more effective our approach to financial engineering.

1. BEST   Incremental costs of proposed projects based on firm quotes, engineers' estimates, etc.

2.   Cost/revenue relationships based on past performance.

3.   Cost/revenue relationships based on consultants' studies or similar.

4. WORST   Market share estimates or some other future external achievement estimates.

2. The users of financial information and their perspectives

Earlier, we briefly touched on accounts which are required by law (statutory accounts) and management information which is reported in management accounts.

> *Statutory accounts* are defined by law and are aimed at public users. In essence, they report on the managers' (directors') stewardship of the business to a wide-ranging public audience.

> *Management accounts* are used by the managers (directors) to run the business, and in the United Kingdom are not subject to any detailed statutory rules.

Statutory accounts

Statutory accounts, which are often called financial accounts, are required by law for limited liability companies (see Chapter 9). Such companies are required by statute to prepare annual financial statements that contain a certain minimum level of information. These reporting requirements and formats are defined by legislation. The detailed legal requirements which specify the extent of information which is to be presented are currently set out in the Companies Act 1985 and in statements of accounting practice published from time to time by the accountancy profession. Additional requirements will arise for a listed company, since it will have to conform with the rules set out in the Stock Exchange listing agreement. In the United Kingdom those financial accounts are subject to review or audit by independent outsiders (the auditors), who must attest to their general truthfulness. They must also be filed at a central registry, called Companies House, where they are available for public inspection.

The prime purpose of published, statutory accounts is to report annually to the existing shareholders the worth of their business and the results of the directors' managerial efforts over the past year.

However, those accounts are also used by others:

- by potential investors, to determine whether they should invest;
- by providers of funds, such as banks, to determine permissible levels of funding, compliance with loan covenants, etc;
- by employees, to formulate wage claims, to determine employer performance and to judge security of employment;
- by creditors, to evaluate risk of non-recovery of credit extended;
- by customers, to determine security of supply;
- by competitors, to evaluate strengths and weaknesses, and to compare performance;
- by the Inland Revenue, as part of the tax collection process;
- by potential acquirors, by regulatory bodies, by Trade Unions and many others.

Each of these audiences is interested more in the one segment of the data presented which is relevant to them than in any other; and for each of these audiences that segment of principal interest will be different.

Management accounts

These accounts are produced within the business every budget period. They should be sufficiently detailed to enable action to be taken if they reveal problems of one kind or another. Generally they are kept confidential because they would be very useful to competitors!

The design and contents of management accounts are completely the responsibility of management. Thus they vary from business to business, to suit the demands of specific individual sections of the business, or of individual responsibility areas (responsibility accounting). Management accounts should highlight areas of specific vulnerability or importance. Actual results are compared to predetermined estimates and budgeted performance. From these comparisons it is possible to identify at an early stage those areas of the business which are not operating according to plan.

To be of any use management accounts must demonstrate a number of features:

- they should be specifically tailored to suit the decision-making needs of each responsible business unit;
- they should look forward to anticipated results as well as reporting historical information;
- they should present an overall simple summary of business performance, with sufficient depth and traceability to enable correlation of cause with effect;
- they should be understood by general management.

As we have already seen, management accounts are a small element of corporate planning and budgetary control systems. In a simplified diagrammatic form, management accounts viewed as a control system can be portrayed as follows:

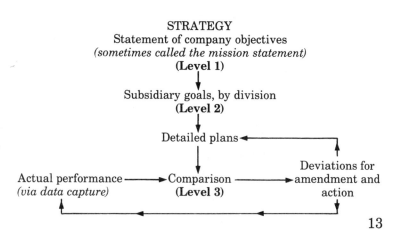

STRATEGY
Statement of company objectives
(sometimes called the mission statement)
(Level 1)

Subsidiary goals, by division
(Level 2)

Detailed plans

Actual performance *(via data capture)* ➝ Comparison **(Level 3)** ➝ Deviations for amendment and action

Management accounts provide different information at different levels of reporting. At top management level (Level 1), control must be exercised over the general direction and flow of the total business entity, and the way in which that performance translates into returns for the providers of capital. At divisional level (Level 2), control is much more oriented toward operations and the meeting of divisional goals. Finally, at departmental levels (Level 3), reporting becomes very detailed in nature, so that individual managers can identify cause and effect, and implement specific corrective action.

3. The purpose of profit

One of the most misused or misunderstood pieces of financial information is profit. Now profit is an emotive word in certain sectors of society, and as a result has from time to time been subjected to a great deal of unjustifiable abuse. Generally, the emotion arises because of the application of the "label" approach. Profit is equated to disposable cash in the hands of the owner of the business enterprise. Envy then takes over and drives sentient human beings into paroxysms of glandular indignation.

It is very rare that profit is the same as disposable cash in the hands of the owner or owners of a business. Businesses can make profits and yet find themselves in receivership due to lack of cash. In fact, profit is simply an accounting measure of the increase in net worth of a business between two dates. Net worth can increase because the excess of trading revenues over trading costs finances reductions in borrowing, greater levels of stock or debtors, or any combination of a multitude of changes in business assets.

Conceptually, profit is the entrepreneur's reward for taking risks. Pragmatically, in any business a portion of profits has to be distributed (ie paid) to the providers of capital for that business. Those providers may be banks who typically provide loan capital and who collect interest as their return, or shareholders who have subscribed for ordinary shares and who receive a periodic dividend. Since those shareholders are the actual owners of the business, their return is only partly made up of the dividends which they receive. The rest of their return consists of the increase in value of the business which they own, supported by that element of profits which is retained in the business.

Thus any business must earn sufficient operating profits to:

— meet the demands of its providers of capital:
  - service the interest on borrowed money
  - provide an acceptable level of return to other providers of capital
— maintain internal integrity:
  - finance growth (or, in times of inflation, sustain normal levels of operation)
  - provide adequate financial cushions against risk.

Furthermore, part of these profits must be available in cash on the dates when external payments need to be made.

4. The role of cash

One of the aims of this book is to demonstrate that we, as financial engineers, are not overly concerned with the products made by our businesses. We are much more concerned with the contribution that those products make to the financial condition of our business, and how sales volumes and costs are related. It is amazing how often businessmen measure success by growth in turnover or relative success by relative turnover levels. Growth in turnover does not guarantee financial success. Financially successful products make a substantial contribution to the business in terms of profitability and cash flow. It is not unusual for high turnover products or high volume customers to be financially the least successful.

It is nothing new to say that cash is the lifeblood of a business. Yet profit and loss accounts and balance sheets continue to dominate the thinking of the average reader of financial information. In a previous section, it was stated that it was still a common misconception to think of the profit and loss account as a summary of all cash flows in and out of a business and of the profit as the surplus of cash inflows over cash outflows at any point in time. Unfortunately, in most businesses not all transactions are settled in cash; and not all cash transactions go through the profit and loss account. For instance, money borrowed from a bank certainly does not constitute profit, nor do advance deposits received from customers!

One of the main reasons why cash is not the same as profit is because accountants recognise economic transactions, such as sales or purchases, when goods or services are provided rather than when cash changes hands. In most industries credit is both allowed and received and in most the net difference between credit taken and credit allowed must be financed by the business. However, the timing of the leads and lags differs from trade to trade, and as a result every business has its own individual cash cycle. This cash cycle can be summarised as follows:

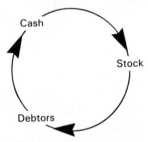

The reader may think that this cycle is simple and obvious, but there are examples of businesses which make money out of little else than taking advantage of the leads and lags in the cash cycle. Consider, for instance, the cash cycle within many cut-price food supermarket chains, where sales are made to retail customers who largely pay cash, and goods are bought on extended credit from long-suffering suppliers. The profit made on the sale of food is miniscule, but that does not concern the supermarket chain overmuch since it makes its money out of the interest earned on the credit taken from its suppliers.

The leads and lags in the cash cycle also limit a business's ability to expand. In a recent report on the causes of the collapse of Nexos, a government-owned office system company, the Parliamentary Accounts Committee stated that the "management tried to do too much, too quickly". The resulting business failure cost the taxpayer £32,000,000.

Growth brings with it a set of very special problems. All too often profitable, rapidly growing companies find themselves short of cash. We may ask why that should happen. It happens, quite simply, because the rate of profit generation is not sufficient to fund the net delay in the cash cycle — the net time lag which arises between the economic transaction (which determines when profit is recorded) and the related cash movement. A company in such a condition is said to be overtrading, and we will look at how that situation arises in a little more detail in Chapter 5.

The upshot is that information about current cash status and future cash flows is vital. So in addition to information about the behaviour of costs and revenues, the financial engineer needs to know about the time leads and lags that are likely to occur in his business between the creation of an asset or liability through a business transaction, and the settlement date for that transaction.

5. A financial engineer's information checklist

We have considered the dangers of lack of information, and the dangers of reading too much into or assigning labels to information which regularly comes to us. But what kind of information do we need to be able to assess the present and future of our businesses validly?

Every business has unique information needs. Yet common to all is the fundamental requirement to know its markets and how to access them, and a need to know its own internal costs. The simplest way of deciding what information is important in your business is to follow a transaction through the business cycle, for example from product design, through manufacture and sale, to collection of cash.

Product design

We are not concerned about the nature of the product. We are concerned about its financial performance. With that in mind we need to be able to assess likely volumes to be achieved by the product in the market-place, and the reaction of the market-place to different price levels. In order to make this kind of evaluation we must understand who our customers are, and what they buy from us. For example:

- Saga holidays specialise in holidays for the over 65s, with features which cover the specific needs of that age group. Clearly, this age group does not suffer from the "school holiday" problem that younger age groups might have to contend with. As a result, better deals in out-of-peak times can be negotiated with, for example, hotel owners.

- British Rail charge commuters (who probably have to travel at specific hours specifically by train — and who are thus a relatively captive market) a higher fare than they charge those travellers who might have the option to travel by other means.

- In its marketing, BMW places stress on "the Ultimate Driving Machine", ie exclusivity and performance. This enables them to charge a price commensurate with that image.

- Many manufacturers in the textile industry have no independent existence of their own as far as the ultimate users of their products are concerned. Their customers (in many cases, customer) are the retail chains to whom they sell. The success or failure of such businesses depends heavily on the efficiency of integration between their production and the retailer. In other words, they have to make the quality specified by the retailer at the price decreed by him, and deliver at the time he specifies.

Manufacture

Again, we are not concerned with the detail of how the product works, in either a functional sense, or in a production engineering sense. We are concerned with knowing what our costs are, and that means knowing which costs are fixed, which are variable, and which change in some other way. For example:

- at a small engineering company which had the opportunity to quote for a one-off sizeable order it was stated that to secure the order, it would have to quote at below cost. On investigation, it turned out that the definition of cost which was being used included overheads, which were all fixed, and which therefore would all be incurred anyway. Thus it became apparent that for this specific order only, a quote below the apparent full cost (but above the direct cost of all the variables) would improve the bottom line;

- costs are not only linked to manufacture and the related cost of manufacturing facilities. Depth of stock carried incurs costs but provides a better level of service to the customer. At a specialist division of a major US industrial company we looked at warehousing policies and customer needs and found a complete absence of information on the levels of stock carried, its usage, the related costs and the degree of customer satisfaction. Nobody knew whether the right balance was being achieved between cost and customer service;

- in certain industries, as discussed earlier, taking an extended period of credit from suppliers may be the key to profitability.

Sale and cash collection

Sales terms can be a strong marketing tool. But many are the times the financial director (engineer?) looks despairingly at his sales colleague as the latter lists sales made "with 2% discount for payment within 10 days". He knows full well that this discount is more expensive than borrowing the money or even factoring the debts, and that the customer will take the discount as well as 12 or more days to pay, and will henceforth demand the same treatment evermore.

The time-honoured alternative to this treatment is to sell on extended credit terms (with possibly a devastating effect on cashflow — not to speak of the enhanced risk of bad debts). Naturally, that costs money, but very often that cost disappears (along with the 2% early settlement discount in a welter of other discounts and commissions) and thus management cannot judge whether or not it is appropriate to do business in this way. In these cases information needs to be gathered linking cause and effect. For example:

- cashflow was deteriorating at a medium-sized manufacturer of capital equipment, while profitability had apparently increased. On investigation it was found that due to extensive part-shipments, spares invoices were leaving the works up to six months later than the main initial spares shipment. In some cases, no invoices had ever been sent! Here was a clear instance of an information gap. The solution was simple and soon put into effect. Henceforth, invoices were sent out for each shipment at the time of despatch of that shipment;

- in a substantial merchandising trade, salesmen's commissions were based on quantities sold, rather than money collected. Discounts were extensively granted contrary to published sales terms, and the company had difficulty chasing customers for what they owed. Following a review of the situation, the terms for salesmen's commissions were revised, with the commission payable now being based on collections rather than on sales. Average sales prices achieved on products rose a little, but the collection period improved dramatically. Some customers were lost, but they were the marginal ones where profitability on sales was small, after discounts and financing costs. In this case, action (payment to salesmen) was linked to the correct cause.

Different businesses have different needs for information. Size, market sector and nature of trade all play a part in determining information needs. But repeating the earlier message that to be able to apply successfully the financial engineering techniques discussed in the following Chapters, the financial engineer needs to be thoroughly conversant with the properties of the information available to him. He needs to know what information he needs, where it can be obtained, its accuracy and its suitability for his purpose — and if it is insufficient or inadequate, he needs to take steps to correct that situation. Otherwise, all his engineering skills will be wasted.

Chapter 2

Accounting concepts and techniques

The previous Chapter reviewed the general nature and attributes of financial information. This Chapter considers how business events are transformed into financial information, and how that financial information is captured and summarised.

1. Business entities

In order to accumulate valid information about performance, every business is regarded as having a separate existence of its own. Often, businesses are sub-divided further for management purposes into units which are capable of performing and reporting meaningfully on their own. Thus business entities fall into two main classifications:

- business entities defined by law, such as partnerships or limited liability companies;
- business entities created by management for purposes of exercising management control, such as profit centres or cost centres.

These two classifications are not mutually exclusive, and in many business organisations legal entity sub-divisions are also profit centres.

The powers, rights and constitutions of legally-defined entities vary from country to country. However, there are three generic types of legally-defined entity used by business organisations worldwide:

- sole traders;
- partnerships (including limited partnerships);
- limited liability companies.

Sole traders

- one person owns and runs the business;
- the owner is completely responsible in law for the business and its debts, ie there is no distinction in law between the owner's personal assets and those of the business.

Most small businesses (the corner grocer, the self-employed plasterer) operate as sole traders.

Partnerships

- two or more persons carry on a business in common with a view to making a profit;
- all partners are legally responsible for the business and for the payment of its debts (the partner's personal asset situation is very similar to that of a sole trader);
- the relationship between partners is set out in a partnership or similar legally binding agreement;
- the liability of some of the partners may be limited, provided they do not take an active part in the management of the business.

Most professional firms, such as accountants, consulting engineers and solicitors operate as partnerships.

Limited liability companies

- a company is treated by law as a separate person (ie its owners may change but the company will continue to exist unaltered);
- each limited company has shareholders who are its owners;
- the rules which govern the relationships and rights of the shareholders are set out formally in a legally binding agreement;
- the objectives and powers of the company are set out formally in a legally binding agreement;

- the company's liability is limited. Consequently, the liability of the shareholders of the company is restricted to the amounts they have paid (or promised to pay) in respect of the company's shares;
- the company has an obligation to produce annual accounts which have been audited by independent, qualified accountants.

Most businesses of any size are incorporated with limited liability. By using the limited liability business vehicle, entrepreneurs can control and limit their risk. At the same time, shares in the business can be sold to raise funds. However, it should be noted that personal guarantees, which are often requested by banks to secure their lending, may reduce or eliminate the limitation on liability. It should also be borne in mind that under certain circumstances the new provisions of the Insolvency Act 1985 will serve to make directors of insolvent limited liability companies personally responsible for the debts of those companies.

A particularly important type of limited liability company is the public limited liability company (or PLC). The PLC is the legal entity vehicle which has to be used when a company's shares are available to be traded by the public. The PLC has all of the attributes outlined above for limited liability companies, but additionally has to conform to the rules and regulations which are determined by the Stock Exchange as applying to its particular status.

Chapter 9, *Published Accounts,* deals further with the characteristics of limited liability companies. Chapters 3 and 10 deal with raising funds and the stock markets.

2. Principles of book-keeping

Book-keeping is the language of accountancy, with a very specific framework and terminology. Book-keeping might be defined as the recording, summarisation and reporting of all business transactions in money terms. But even this simple definition warrants closer and more careful scrutiny. The following practical questions arise:

- what is the trigger which defines that a transaction has happened?
- how can we be sure that all triggered transactions are recorded?
- how do we know that the right value has been assigned to each transaction?

When does a transaction happen?

The timing of most transactions would seem to be obvious. The bag of apples changing hands in return for some coins quite clearly indicates that ownership has passed and a recordable transaction has taken place. But consider what happens if those apples are sold on credit, and the seller retains title to them until he is paid. Ownership has not passed — but a transaction of some kind has undoubtedly occurred.

Similarly, if you are in business building destroyers, hotels, or anything which takes more than a year to complete, you know that it is unfair and unreasonable to record no sales activity until those large capital items are fully and finally ready to be handed over to their future owners. But on the other hand, any sales that you record before those items are ready are bound to be a fiction (since it is not possible to sell half a destroyer) — so on what underlying transactions should you base your sales reports?

Yet the timing of transactions is a vital component of the assessment of performance and the determination of ownership of business assets.

The events which determine whether or not a transaction has happened are governed by a blend of accounting conventions and legal practice. In general, a sale is recognised when goods are despatched, or services are provided. On long-term contracts, special provisions apply, which allow for a proportional booking of profit depending on the likelihood of final outcome and the stage of completion of the job. Similarly, purchases are recognised when goods or services are received. Where goods are bought under retention of title terms (otherwise called *Romalpa* clauses), general practice is to recognise receipt, but to make clear that that element of stock is strictly speaking not the company's property.

The importance of knowing the conventions adopted becomes apparent if you consider the following examples:

Assessing performance

A smallish manufacturing company which had been funded by the Government had developed a novel form of military watercraft. Build time approximated 15 months. For its first published statutory accounts, the company decided to take a proportion of profit for those vessels which were partially built at the year-end. It reported a healthy income for that period. Unfortunately, when it came to sea trials and commissioning, the vessels proved to be less than successful, and extensive unforeseen work (and expense) proved necessary to make them seaworthy. As a result, the published statutory accounts of the second year showed a substantial loss.

When trying to evaluate the performance of this company for potential investors (or for that matter for the company's existing banker) the first thing to do was to discard the financial information shown in the published statutory accounts. Instead, a meaningful presentation of data had to be designed, and the relevant information gathered. Specific information had to be obtained on the profitability of individual watercraft, from beginning of build, to sale 15 months later. In fact, that information showed that all but the first two craft were built at an overall profit, and furthermore, that the later builds were more profitable than the earlier. This message was rather different from the one presented in the statutory accounts of a profit turning into a loss!

It is worth pointing out that, almost perversely, cashflow in the first (supposedly profitable) period was adverse (as money was being spent on the build of the watercraft), and that cashflow in the second (loss-making) year was positive, as one by one the vessels were sold.

Determining security

A medium-sized metal manufacturing company was entering a period of rapid growth and requested increased funding facilities from its bank. The bank was willing to co-operate, but required security. The company was prepared to accept, among other things, a floating charge on their stock. Matters progressed for a while, a sharp recession set in, and the company became insolvent. The bank sent in a receiver, who very soon found out that most of the stock (which constituted a substantial part of the bank's security) did not belong to the company, but belonged to its supplier under a retention of title clause. Much litigation ensued.

Recording all transactions

The basic ingredient of book-keeping is the methodology of double entry. This approach to record-keeping recognises that there are two aspects to each transaction:

- the acquisition of rights or assets,

  in return for

- the depletion of cash, the incurring of a liability or the consumption of an asset.

Thus double entry book-keeping involves reflecting in the books of account each business transaction as a set of two book-keeping entries. For example:

When a businessman starts up in business he will normally open a separate business bank account and start it off with some of his own money (say £100,000). The business will then have an asset (cash in the bank) and a liability to pay back the money lent by the owner to the business.

The accounting entry to record this transaction is:

Debit: Cash at bank   £100,000
    Credit: Owner's capital account
        or share capital   £(100,000)

The financial state of any business may be summarised in the form of a balance sheet. The balance sheet is a "photograph" at one point in time of the assets and liabilities of the business, and of its capital. Thus the balance sheet of the above business, at the point where it is just about to start, is:

Cash (or net assets)	£100,000
Capital (ie due to owner)	£(100,000)

After the original injection of capital by the owner, the business may well borrow funds in order to be better placed to buy stock and machinery. For example:

In order to finance the acquisition of premises, the business described above borrows £50,000 from the bank on a long-term loan. It also spends £65,000, which is payable in 45 days time, on machinery, and £20,000 paid in cash, on stocks of raw materials.

The accounting entries to record these transactions will be:

Debit: Fixed assets — premises	£50,000
Credit: Due to bank long term	£(50,000)
Debit: Fixed assets — machinery	£65,000
Credit: Creditors	£(65,000)
Debit: Stocks	£20,000
Credit: Cash	£(20,000)

The balance sheet of the business (which has not yet commenced to trade) will be as follows:

Fixed assets		
— premises	£50,000	
— machinery	£65,000	£115,000
Stocks		£20,000
Cash		£80,000
		£100,000
Creditors		£(115,000)
Net assets		£100,000
Capital (ie due to owner)		£(100,000)

The transactions described above only changed the composition of the net assets of the business. Because of that, they did not affect the net asset position or the capital. However, when a business starts to trade (ie to make sales and incur costs) the net result will be a profit or a loss. That profit or loss will increase or decrease the net assets of the business. Since the net assets are payable to the owners of the business, the capital amount payable to them will be affected. For example:

> In the case of the company which we are using as an example, sales for the first month were £15,000 of finished product which cost £7,500, all of which was drawn from stock. All sales were made on credit and were receivable in 30 days. The company also incurred wage costs of £1,000, which were paid in cash.
>
> The accounting entries to record these transactions will be:

Debit:	Debtors	£15,000
Credit:	Sales	£(15,000)
Debit:	Cost of sales	£7,500
Credit:	Stocks	£(7,500)
Debit:	Wages expense	£1,000
Credit:	Cash	£(1,000)

The balance sheet of the business will be as follows:

Fixed assets		
— premises	£50,000	
— machinery	£65,000	£115,000
Stocks		£12,500
Debtors		£15,000
Cash		£79,000
		£106,500
Creditors		£(115,000)
Net assets		£106,500
Original capital		£(100,000)
Profit		£(6,500)
		£(106,500)

The dual nature of accounting entries leads to the following simple accounting equation:

$$ASSETS = LIABILITIES$$

or, in a more useful form,

Gross assets — Gross liabilities incurred by the business
=
Net assets
=
Shareholders' funds (owed by the business to the shareholders)

Because of double entry the two sides of the equation are equal no matter what changes occur in the composition of the assets and liabilities.

Since each side of a double entry can be independently verified, the mechanism of double entry in itself can give considerable basic assurance that all transactions are being processed. To put it simply, if the balance sheet and profit and loss do not balance, then some transactions have not been properly processed.

There are, of course, many other more sophisticated financial controls which can be installed to ensure that data capture is comprehensive and accurate. Perhaps the most important financial control is that exercised by management itself — either directly, through review and query, or indirectly by means of an internal audit function.

Assigning value to transactions

Most transactions have an easily identifiable value. The sale of finished product and the purchase of stock for an agreed price are familiar transactions where unit revenues and costs should be easy to assess. Yet even in these apparently straightforward areas difficulties can arise. For example:

> Intertrade Limited purchases 10,000 glo-form toys at £5 each, and sells 5,000 almost immediately for £9 each. The branch manager hurriedly re-orders another 10,000, but has to pay a higher price of £6. The company then sells another 5,000 at £10 each. What is the profit made by Intertrade Limited, and what is the residual cost of stock?
>
> Answer: 5,000 glo-toys sold at £9 and 5,000 glo-toys sold at £10 each gives revenue of £95,000. The cost is 10,000 at £5 (£50,000), or 5,000 at £5 and 5,000 at £6 (£55,000), or possibly 5,000 at £5 and 5,000 at £5.50 (£52,500). The

profit is £45,000, or £40,000, or £42,500 respectively. The cost of the residual stock is £60,000, or £55,000, or £57,500. It all depends on whether old stock is sold before new stock. In many businesses where stock cannot be differentiated, profit and the value of the residual stock depend on what cost flow assumption is adopted in calculating the cost of sales. As can be seen from this example, the amounts involved can be significant.

In order to introduce some degree of uniformity into the reporting of financial information, accountants have agreed on a limited number of fundamental accounting concepts, and on a further number of standard accounting practices.

Standard accounting practices are set out in Appendix 1 and will be reviewed generally in Chapter 9. The fundamental accounting concepts, of which there are four, are as follows:

- *Going concern — basis for measurement*
  The going concern assumption defines the conditions under which business assets (and liabilities) are assigned values. Business assets are assigned values assuming that the business will continue for the foreseeable future.

  Clearly, under normal conditions, the valuation placed on business assets is likely to be much higher while the business continues than if the assets were to be sold individually. For example, expensive specialised plant and machinery might have little or no resale value. Partially finished products might be worthless. Some assets, such as prepaid rates or advertising, or advance corporation tax may not be realisable. Even freehold property might have to be sold at a loss, if disposed of under forced sale conditions. At the same time lease penalty clauses, redundancy costs, and unprovided deferred taxation might crystallise and reduce net assets further.

  Financial statements do not normally concern themselves with the break-up value of businesses: but for most businesses, break-up valuation is likely to be very much lower than valuation on a going concern basis. For that reason, when evaluating the security cover available within a business, bankers significantly reduce the net book value of most specialised business assets and ask for valuations on those assets where market values exist.

- *Accruals — measurement of performance*

  This assumption deals with the need to match costs and revenues in order to show properly the results of operations for any given period; ie for accounting purposes revenue reported in the period should be compared with the costs and expenses of earning that revenue, rather than with the cash spends made during that period. In other words, the reported profit should show how efficiently the resources of the business have been applied.

  Financial statements reflect the results of sales made during the period and the related costs whether or not those costs have been invoiced or paid.

- *Consistency — measurement of performance*

  A business should be consistent with its accounting treatment of items where alternatives are available. Once a business has chosen a specific accounting policy for dealing with items this method should be used consistently for all items in that class. In this way users of financial statements can draw meaningful conclusions from reported results.

  Financial statements are prepared consistently, so that they give a meaningful picture of performance over time.

- *Prudence — recognition of income*

  Revenues and profits are not deemed to occur until the likelihood of realisation is high. However, anticipated losses should be provided for unless wholly unlikely to occur.

  Financial statements are prepared diligently and cautiously.

3. Calculation of accounting profit

In the previous Chapter it was indicated that it was the basic objective of each business to earn a return for the owners of that business. Profit was also defined as an accounting measure of the increase in net worth of a business between two dates. The importance of profit stems from the fact that it is the measure of the return made by the business for its shareholders. However, profit is not intended to be a measure of the amount of cash available for distribution to those shareholders. For that reason, the calculation of profit is based on executed transactions (that is to say, sales made which are contractually binding, and costs incurred) irrespective of the related cash position. Profit is computed applying the accruals concept discussed in the previous section.

A normal trading business makes profit by selling goods or supplying services at prices in excess of the costs at which they were purchased or made. Other expenses are incurred in running a business, such as selling and administration. Those expenses must be met out of income in order to arrive at net profit. In addition, the business will most probably acquire and use fixed assets, whose cost must be allocated against income.

The aggregate value of goods despatched or services rendered in a period is the *revenue* of the business for the period. The aggregate value of the costs incurred in despatching those goods or supplying those services for that same period is the *expense* related to that particular parcel of revenues.

Although revenues relate to specific supplies, expenses can typically relate to specific supplies or to the passage of time. For example, the expenses of a motor distributor who sold 6 cars in a month would be made up of the specific cost to him of the vehicles plus the time-related cost of maintaining his showroom and his salesmen. If in one month he sold no cars at all, he would still have incurred expenses relating to the showroom and the salesmen.

Because some costs relate intimately to revenues, and others have no connection with revenues but relate to the passing of time, it is convenient to define profit at two different levels:

- *Gross profit*, defined as revenue less the direct cost of goods sold;
- *Net profit*, defined as revenue less all expenses.

In effect, this classification separates the generally repetitive and usually individually lesser costs which are incurred directly in connection with creating saleable product from the generally infrequent but normally larger costs of creating and maintaining the business's capacity to function. This distinction is important, and is a fundamental building block in developing a financial model for any business.

Gross profit —

Revenues	X
Less direct product or service costs (cost of sales)	(X)
Gross profit	X

Direct product or service costs will typically include materials used in production, wages (and wage on-costs such as National Insurance), energy used in production and so on. These costs are specifically identifiable with units of output.

Net profit —

Revenues	X
Less direct product or service costs (cost of sales)	(X)
Gross profit	X
Costs of functional capacity	(X)
Net profit	XX

Besides indirect production costs such as factory rent, rates and insurance, the costs of functional capacity include the cost of the sales force and general and administrative expenses. All of these costs are incurred in order to create an environment in which the product can be made and sold. In effect, these are the costs of the infrastructure of the business.

4. The balance sheet

A balance sheet is a photograph of the business at a point in time, with shareholders' funds, or sources of capital, equalling net assets.

One side of the balance sheet shows the sources of capital and where they originate from:

- share capital supplied by the shareholders;
- profit retained from the profits of the business;
- revaluation surpluses arising on the increase in value of long-term assets held by the business.

The other side of the balance sheet shows the net assets which are being funded by the capital at one specific point in time. Net assets are themselves composed of different types of assets and liabilities. In order to make the balance sheet summary as meaningful as possible the assets and liabilities are classified according to their nature:

- *Current assets* are assets held for resale or conversion into cash. Such assets are also known as circulating assets, since they are continuously being sold and replaced. Typically, these include cash, debtors and stocks.
- *Current liabilities* are amounts owed by the business and which will become due for payment within the 12 months following the balance sheet date. Trade creditors, wages and certain types of taxation are the most common current liabilities.
- *Fixed assets* are those assets held for use in the business rather than for resale or conversion into cash. Examples include buildings, machinery and equipment.
- *Long term liabilities* are amounts owed but due for payment more than 12 months after the balance sheet date. Mortgages and bank loans are the most common examples.

These classifications are important since they form the basis on which bankers and others judge the liquidity of a business.

The money amount that needs to be invested in stock and

debtors is reduced by the amount of credit that can be taken from suppliers. Hence, the net of current assets and current liabilities represents the net amount which is funding routine trading assets and which is continually circulating on the cash-to-stock-to-debtors-to-cash loop illustrated in Chapter 1. This net circulating capital of the business is called the *working capital.* This term will be used frequently in the Chapters which follow. Working capital is further discussed in Chapter 5.

5. The cash flow effects of accounting conventions

It has been stated earlier that the profit made by a business does not necessarily equal the cash generated by that business since credit transactions and non-cash items introduce lags and leads between accounting profit and available cash.

Having reviewed double entry book-keeping and the accounting methodology behind the profit and loss statement we are now in a position to consider in detail the principal leads and lags which cause differences between profit and cash-flow. Principal transactions and their associated double-entry book-keeping entries are as follows:

	Book-keeping	P/L effect	Cash effect
Sales made on credit	Dr Receivables (b/s) Cr Sales (p/l)	X	No
Receipt of money from debtors	Dr Cash (b/s) Cr Receivables (b/s)	No	X
Purchases of stock	Dr Inventory (b/s) Cr Cash (b/s)	No	X
Purchases of equipment	Dr Fixed assets (b/s) Cr Cash (b/s)	No	X
Purchase of services for future periods	Dr Prepayments (b/s) Cr Cash (b/s)	No	X
Assumption of liability attributable to current period but due for payment in future period	Dr Expenses (p/l) Cr Payables (b/s)	X	No
Depreciation	Dr Expenses (p/l) Cr Fixed assets (b/s)	X	No
Long-term borrowing	Dr Cash (b/s) Cr Long-term debt (b/s)	No	X

b/s means balance sheet   p/l means profit and loss statement

In capital-intensive trades, the effect of depreciation is particularly significant because of the large investment in fixed assets (see below).

6. Depreciation and amortisation

Fixed assets such as buildings, vehicles, plant and machinery, are held by the business and used with the objective of earning revenue. Fixed assets are used and contribute to profits over many accounting periods. In order to measure performance properly the profit and loss account must be a statement of revenue earned and expenses incurred in the specific accounting period which is being reported on. Consequently, methods need to be adopted to compute the business cost of the consumption of each fixed asset during the period in question.

The total cost of the fixed asset is nothing to do with the expenses of any individual period of account. On acquisition of the asset, that cost is capitalised in the balance sheet. This cost is then apportioned over the period during which the asset is in productive service using some suitable basis such as time, or throughput. The amount of apportionment made in each period is known as depreciation or amortisation. Amortisation involves the same principles as depreciation; it is usually used in connection with intangible assets such as expenditure incurred for the benefit of future periods.

In general, during its total life the value to the business of an asset will decrease. At the date at which an asset is disposed of it may have a residual or saleable value. Therefore over the asset's life the business will have used an amount equal to the original cost less any value recovered at disposal. The term "original cost" may include such costs as purchase price plus any labour or costs incurred in bringing the asset to its present state or location (including, where appropriate, interest).

In order to calculate how much depreciation is charged in a period we must know or estimate the following:

(i) cost;

(ii) the estimated useful life of the asset;
(iii) the residual value at the end of its useful life;
(iv) the basis upon which the cost should be allocated.

The amount of depreciation to be charged over the useful life of an asset will be (i) minus (iii). The amount of depreciation to be charged in any one period will depend upon which allocation method is adopted. Many methods exist, the two most common being based on time apportionment on either a straight line or a reducing balance basis.

Straight line apportionment allocates (i) minus (iii) over the number of periods in the estimated useful life, whereas the reducing balance basis writes off a certain percentage of cost in the first year. In the second year the same percentage is applied to the original cost less the amount written off in the previous year, ie the reduced balance. This process is continued in future years.

Example: Cost = £4,000,000
               Useful life = 4 years
               Residual/saleable value = £2,000,000

(i) *Straight line method (£000s)*

$$\frac{\text{Cost} - \text{residual value}}{\text{Useful life}} = \frac{4,000 - 2,000}{4} = 500 \, \text{pa}$$

(ii) *Reducing balance (£000s)*

Cost − residual value = 2,000

Therefore since the useful life is 4 years we require a percentage which when applied to the original cost over 4 years leaves a value of 2,000.

Using a depreciation rate of approximately 15% we get (£000s):

Original cost	4,000
Less 15%	(600)
	3,400
Less 15%	(510)
	2,890
Less 15%	(434)

	2,456
Less 15%	(368)
Value at end	2,088

(Difference due to rounding to 15%)

Straight line allocation is more appropriate where equal benefit is derived over the useful life, eg buildings. The reducing balance basis is more appropriate where a greater benefit is derived from the asset in the earlier years of its life, eg machinery which provides more productive hours when new than when old.

The method and rate of depreciation chosen will usually be decided in terms of a general policy for a group of assets, eg plant and vehicles, rather than on a specific basis for each individual asset. These general policies are then applied to each specific asset.

It should be noted that depreciation based on historic purchase cost allocates the cost incurred in creating the asset over the period during which it is in use. It is not a method of providing a fund to replace the asset at the end of its useful life.

Chapter 3

Sources of funds and cost of capital

A business may fund its operations from a great many different sources. Clearing banks, merchant banks, the Stock Exchange, venture capital firms and so on are willing providers of funds for businesses which suit their tastes. Among this selection of potential suppliers of finance are those who will suit the business better in terms of cost, cash flows or amount which they are willing to provide. In other words, appropriate composition of the capital structure is important, since that structure will determine for the business:

- the cost of capital;
- the shareholders' risk;
- the borrowing capacity.

1. The cost of capital

All business organisations justify the capital invested in them from whatever source by earning appropriate returns on that capital. Those which perform successfully and earn high returns are rewarded by being able easily to draw further investment funds from different sources. The penalties for failing to perform are initially a loss of confidence on the part of the providers of capital, followed perhaps by takeover by a more successful business, receivership or liquidation.

Different providers of capital fund in different ways. The greater the degree of risk-taking in the capital provided, the greater are the rewards required by the provider.

Thus businesses have available to them sources of capital which vary both in cost and in the rights that the providers have over the assets and trade of the business.

Clearly, the composition of the capital structure of a business will determine the aggregate minimum return which needs to be earned in order to meet the requirements of the providers of funds. That minimum return is termed the cost of capital.

Detailed calculation of the cost of capital is dealt with in Section 5 of this Chapter.

2. Shareholders' risk

A business may fund its operations from internal or external resources. Internal resources are the profit which is kept within the business. External resources include borrowings or the input of capital from the owners.

There are many companies which do not borrow money as a matter of policy. This policy is most often seen in trades of a cyclical nature such as fashion textiles, where one good year can easily be followed by one or more bad ones. Companies which have little or no borrowings are better able to stand losses in bad years, have no worries about covering interest payments or repayment of loans and are better placed to continue to pay dividends to their shareholders. Examples of such companies include Nottingham Manufacturing (which at one time had nearly £100 million in cash and cash equivalents on its balance sheet) and, until recently, Marks & Spencer.

However, companies which have a rigorous no-borrowing policy may find themselves severely constrained when it comes to capital investments. They may be unable to afford to fund from existing cash flow the substantial initial outlay often required for new investment, particularly where the paybacks are likely to arise over a relatively long period of time. For that reason, most companies prefer to perform detailed project appraisal along the lines which will be discussed in Chapter 6. They are then able to assess whether any specific investment project is worthwhile by determining whether the rate of return expected from the project exceeds the cost of borrowed funds by a sufficient margin to provide for risk and profit.

Most businesses use a blend of owners' capital (known as equity) and borrowed money. This reflects the fact that the providers of secured borrowings are normally prepared to accept a modest return in recompense for an absence of risk. As a result, the returns available to the shareholders are increased by the introduction of borrowings, as long as the funding is used for projects which are chosen so that the rate of return exceeds the cost of borrowing.

However, the modest return promised by the business to the lenders of funds must always be paid. The lenders do not regard themselves as providers of risk capital and they want their return whether or not the business has made a profit during the year. Furthermore, that return must be paid in preference to the returns to any other providers of funds, including the shareholders. This order of payout priorities undoubtedly increases the shareholders' risk.

Consider the example below, which demonstrates the combination of enhanced rewards for shareholders coupled with greater risk for them—

> Oakex Limited makes fertilizers and specialised weedkillers. It is a successful and growing company, with a number of interesting and novel new products in the pipeline. During 1985 the company made a profit of £600,000. The capital structure of the business at the end of 1985 was as follows (£000s):
>
> | | |
> |---|---:|
> | Ordinary shares | 2,000 |
> | Retained profit | 1,000 |
> | Capital employed | 3,000 |
>
> In this case, capital employed was all composed of shareholders' funds. Thus, Oakex had a return on shareholders' funds of 20%.
>
> Koaex Limited is a very similar operation in the

same industry, earning the same returns and having a very similar balance sheet. However, Koaex decided in 1984 to expand its manufacturing capacity by borrowing £1,000,000 at a cost of 12% per annum (variable). That capacity came on stream in 1985, and contributed £200,000 to the business before interest costs. The interest costs amounted to £120,000. The profit and loss account of Koaex for the year ended 31 December 1985 was as follows:

Profit from core business (as Oakex)	600
Contribution from new investment	200
Interest	(120)
Net profit	680

The capital structure and profit and loss account of Koaex at the end of 1985 were as follows (000s):

Ordinary shares	2,000
Retained profit	1,000
Shareholders' funds	3,000
Borrowings	1,000
Capital employed	4,000

Thus, Koaex had a return on shareholders' funds of 23%, and the use of borrowings to fund a project which earned more than it cost enhanced the earnings available to the shareholders.

However, in the next year, times were very hard in this industrial sector. New competition from abroad caused margins to fall dramatically, and interest rates increased to 15%.

The respective profit and loss position of each of the two companies was as follows:

Oakex, net profit available to shareholders	120

Koaex—	
Profit from core business (as Oakex)	120
Contribution from new investment	40
Interest	(150)
Net profit available to shareholders	10

This example illustrates how the priority possessed by lenders of money may consume profits in hard times, and how the use of borrowed money for expansion can render the business dangerously exposed to economic winds and industrial downturns.

Heavy borrowings in a new business where start-up losses are expected can also create enormous risks for the shareholders. Consider Fruex Limited:

> Fruex Limited is a new venture. Stocks and other working capital needs of £10,000 are funded by the owners. Fixed assets with a life of ten years and a cost of £10,000 are funded by a long-term bank loan, the first instalment of which is due at the end of the first year of trade. The owners expect a loss of £9,000 in the first year, a profit of £9,000 in the second year, and a profit of £20,000 in the third year.
>
> The initial balance sheets are as follows—

	Opening	First year
Working capital	10,000	1,000
Fixed assets	10,000	9,000
	20,000	10,000
Borrowings	(10,000)	(9,000)
Net assets	10,000	1,000
Share capital	10,000	10,000
Profit and loss	–	(9,000)
	10,000	1,000

> The crucial measure at the end of the first year from the bank's point of view is the relationship between bank funds and those of the shareholders. At the first year end the bank has lent Fruex £9,000 but the owners' capital has been eroded by the losses down to £1,000. That relationship demonstrates that this company is effectively the bank trading as Fruex Limited. Not many banks would support a company in this position.

This example shows that if losses are expected, in order to minimise risk, the relationship between shareholders' funds and bank borrowings should be measured at the worst anticipated point to determine whether that relationship remains at a level which is still acceptable to the bank. If that relationship is not acceptable, then steps should be taken to enhance the company's borrowing capacity or to introduce new outside ordinary shareholders. There is a further example of this unfortunate but all too common occurrence in Chapter 8.

3. Borrowing capacity

Factors which limit borrowing capacity

The Oakex and Fruex examples illustrate the importance of maintaining an appropriate relationship between borrowing and shareholders' funds. That relationship is termed balance-sheet gearing, and may be defined as:

Borrowings : Shareholders' funds

All banks use this relationship as one of their measures of the borrowing capacity of a business. What constitutes an appropriate level of gearing varies from business to business. Commodity traders and property development companies have very high levels of gearing—many times greater than shareholders' funds. A manufacturing company would normally be regarded as being fully borrowed if its borrowings matched its shareholders' funds, and in most cases borrowings should run at about half of shareholders' funds. It is obvious that too low a level of borrowings may result in missed earnings opportunities, whereas too high a level can be a dangerous drain on resources if market conditions become difficult.

A further and similar indicator of the appropriateness of borrowing levels is profit and loss gearing. That is defined as:

Interest cost : Operating profit before interest and tax

This indicator is also called interest cover (ie the number of times that interest can be paid out of the pre-interest profits). Once again, there is no absolute hard-and-fast rule. The required level of cover varies but in a normal steady business an acceptable level would probably be two times cover or better.

The two indicators outlined above, together with security cover for the principal which is borrowed, constitute the main tangible measures with which banks gauge the borrowing capacity of businesses. One further vital but intangible measure is the credibility with which management are viewed at the bank.

Increasing borrowing capacity

Borrowings can be entered into in a great variety of ways, and in recent years banks and merchant banks have been anxious to create a great many different options so as to suit the needs of their customers and increase borrowing capacity. Methods of borrowing include:

- overdrafts;
- mortgages;
- sale and leaseback of property;
- acceptance credits;
- factoring;
- leasing;
- specialist off-balance sheet borrowing;
- issue of debentures.

Overdrafts: Overdrafts are perhaps the most common form of bank lending. They may be secured or unsecured, but their main feature is that they are specifically designed to support current business transactions rather than the acquisition of long-term assets. Therefore, overdrafts should be self-liquidating, ie they should be subject to a continuous process of being paid off and drawn down again as transactions pass through the business.

Overdraft borrowing is usually cheaper than long-term debt since overdrafts give greater liquidity to the bank which can withdraw them at short notice. For that reason it is to each business's advantage to arrange for a proper short-term/long-term split of its financing requirements, paying due regard to the need for the continued availability of long-term funds. The cost of overdraft borrowings is invariably linked to bank rate.

Mortgages: We are all quite familiar with the domestic mortgage, and the commercial mortgage is much the same, although the term is normally shorter. The amount lent is usually restricted to about two-thirds of the market value of the security, the mortgage being secured by a fixed charge on the related land and buildings.

The cost of mortgage borrowings is usually linked to bank base rate, and because the lender commits funds for a long time, that cost is normally higher than the cost of an overdraft.

Sale and leaseback of property: The sale and lease-back was developed as a way of releasing capital otherwise locked up in the freehold properties owned by businesses. In this situation, a business sells its freehold or leasehold interest in its premises to an institution at full market value, but continues to occupy those premises and to pay a market rent.

In effect, such a deal is an alternative to mortgage finance. As such, it may be attractive to businesses which anticipate strong profitability in the future but which currently require rather more funds than can be generated through a mortgage. This is because mortgages are restricted to about two-thirds of market value whereas the sale proceeds of a sale and lease-back should approximate market value. Furthermore, the servicing cost of the mortgage could well be higher than the rental payable under a sale and lease-back. The only drawbacks to the business are the loss of the ownership of the property (and hence the loss of any increase in underlying value), and the fact that rent reviews will eventually push up the rent costs.

Acceptance credits: Acceptance credits are an old established method of financing short-term trading. They involve the drawing of a bill by the borrower which promises to pay a sum of money at a future date (say in three or six months' time). That bill is then accepted (that is, guaranteed) by a bank which is an accepting house. The bill can then be sold in the discount market and will command the best rates. The borrower receives the proceeds of the sale, less an acceptance commission.

This method of funding trade can be very cost-effective.

Interest rates are linked to the cost of wholesale money on the money markets which is very often less than the cost of an equivalent conventional bank overdraft. However, the amounts drawn need to be substantial.

Factoring: There are a number of forms which factoring can take, but in essence it involves either the direct sale of debtors to a third party, or an assignment of those debtors to that party in return for a cash advance. Because of the more detailed level of monitoring which factoring companies are able to undertake (as compared to clearing banks) funds advanced as a proportion of the underlying security are typically greater. Thus the great advantage of this form of debtor funding is that the borrowing capacity of most companies can be increased.

Non-recourse factoring is the simplest form. This is an arrangement whereby the factor simply buys book debts outright and accepts the full risk of bad debts himself. Since the debt belongs to the factor, he also assumes responsibility for maintenance of the sales ledger, collection and credit control (typically, credit limits are established for each of the company's customers by the factor). Non-recourse factoring tends to be expensive because of the assumption of bad debt risk by the factor.

Factoring can be less expensive if the company is prepared to retain the bad debt risk. Recourse factoring is an arrangement similar to the above, except that the vendor of the debtors undertakes to repay to the factor any losses arising as a result of bad debts.

Both of the above arrangements involve the sale of specific debtors to the factor, who, in addition to finance, provides a debt collection service. The alternative method of using debtors to raise funds is to borrow specifically against the security of book debts without provision of any other service. This kind of arrangement is termed block or invoice discounting, and there are a number of ways in which it can be done.

In the case of block discounting, the factor will enter into an agreement with the company to provide finance up to an agreed percentage of approved debts (usually 80%). In addition, an overriding absolute limit to funds provided will also apply. The company will then provide the factor with copy invoices and other evidence of sales whereupon he will pay over the agreed percentage advance. The administration of the sales ledger remains with the company, and status returns in the form of aged listings of debtors are made periodically to the factor. In addition, the company acts as trustee and collects the debts on behalf of the factor. In practice, if monthly returns are made, at each month end the company either remits or receives 80% of the net movement of its approved debts.

Invoice discounting is a similar arrangement, except that individual invoices are involved, rather than blocks of debtors.

The main advantage of block discounting arrangements is that customers will probably remain unaware that factoring is in place, since payment is made directly to the company.

Leasing: Strictly speaking leasing is a form of hire, whereby all of the benefits of ownership of the asset (typically an item of plant or equipment) are enjoyed by the user although the legal form of ownership does not pass to him. Within this broad framework, leasing may be written in a variety of shapes, varying in terms of payment pattern and risk to the lender (lessor).

A finance lease is structured so that the rentals payable during the primary lease term fully cover the capital cost of the equipment, as well as giving the lessor the level of interest which provides him with a satisfactory profit. The primary period often correlates with the useful life of the asset, but it is normal to provide for a subsequent further secondary lease period at a peppercorn rent in case the asset continues to be of use. From the lessor's point of view at the end of the primary lease period the equipment is completely paid for. As a result, there is no terminal risk in his hands, and this is reflected in the interest rates charged on such a lease.

· An operating lease is normally written for a period which is substantially shorter than the useful working life of the asset. As a result, it is expected that there will be a residual value attaching to the asset at the conclusion of the lease term. The lease payments reflect the full interest charge, but include only the amortisation of the capital depreciation over the lease term. In these circumstances, the lessor is at risk, since he depends on ultimate achievement of the realisation values estimated at inception of the lease. Naturally, this increases the absolute cost of such leases, although as a compensation, the cash flow "cost" of such leases is relatively low.

Leasing can be very beneficial to a business for two significant reasons. Firstly, it matches cash outflows made under the terms of the lease with the cash inflows generated by the leased assets. Secondly, security is confined to the particular asset being purchased, and does not extend to other assets of the business.

Off-balance sheet borrowing: Off-balance sheet borrowings tend to be specialised transactions designed to meet specific business needs. Very often they arise because of a particular need to avoid showing excessive balance sheet gearing. For example, seasonal businesses (such as those involved in agriculture or food processing) may need to fund crops which can only be harvested or purchased at one particular time of year, but which are then sold into the end-user market throughout the year. If they choose to borrow funds on a conventional basis to fund purchase of those crops, then their balance sheet stocks and borrowings will be significantly inflated by that large one-off purchase.

Instead, those businesses might elect to pass those purchases through a merchant bank, which can buy them and retain legal ownership, enabling the company to call off small amounts as needed. Naturally, the merchant bank will require a guarantee that the company concerned will carry the stockholding risk, but the essential element of the deal is that the stock and the borrowings are not located in the company.

Debentures: The term debentures covers a multiplicity of different financial instruments all of which provide evidence of a debt. The debt is usually but not necessarily long-term in nature, secured, and repayable at a specific date or within a range of dates. Debentures may carry a fixed interest rate, or a rate linked to market rate indicators.

In many ways debentures are similar to long-term bank finance. The interest must always be paid, takes precedence over ordinary shareholders' dividends and is tax deductible. However, the flexibility available in the design of debentures can be of great use to the financial engineer. For example, debentures can be issued:

- with fixed interest rate. If those debentures are issued to fund a specific project, then the cost of capital for that project is effectively fixed;

- with conversion rights. The debenture holders may have the right to convert their debentures into ordinary shares on some pre-agreed basis at some pre-arranged date. That may justify the issue of the debentures with a lower than market interest rate;

- with no running yield but with a terminal gain (otherwise known as zero coupon deep discount). Debentures can be issued with no interest rate at all, but with a selling price which is much lower than the redemption value. In that way, the subscribers do not get a running yield but instead receive a substantial cash payment on redemption. This provides the borrower with a much better cash flow position in the short term.

It is usually better to combine a number of these sources. That has the same effect as the dual sourcing of raw materials — it improves supplies in terms of quantity and reliability, and may reduce price. After all, borrowed funds are as much a raw material as steel, oil or any other input with which the business works.

4. Permanent capital

Permanent capital can be characterised by the fact that the providers of that capital are prepared to accept greater risks than the lenders of funds. However, as recompense they expect greater returns. For that reason, permanent capital is more commonly termed equity or risk capital.

In the case of companies limited by shares, the capital put in by the owners is measured in terms of the issued shares. There are different types of share capital which differ in respect of their rights to the equity of the business in different situations:

- *ordinary shares* are the most common type of share in issue. They have equal voting rights and an equal share in the profits and net assets of the company;

- *deferred ordinary shares* are a form of ordinary share which has no rights when it is issued, but which gains those rights when certain previously agreed triggers are reached; eg in a management buy-out, management's deferred shares may convert to ordinaries if forecast targets are achieved;

- *preference shares* normally have a preferential right to a fixed dividend ahead of the ordinary shareholders, and also have a priority right to recover their capital value in the event of liquidation;

- *cumulative preference shares* have an extra right to accumulate passed dividends, and would have arrears of dividend paid to them ahead of any dividends to the ordinary shareholders;

- other forms of share exist — for example "A" or "B" shares which may carry different rights, preferred ordinaries, non-voting shares etc.

Raising permanent capital for unquoted companies

Many independent private companies need to raise capital, whether for expansion, re-equipment or just to enable the company to pay substantial sums to the owners. The borrowing route is relatively easy to pursue, unless the company is already fully borrowed or reluctant (for the reasons previously outlined) to increase or incur borrowings. Usually, the only other viable alternative is to raise some form of permanent capital.

There are a great many different potential sources of

permanent capital funds available to a business, and the nature of the company and the purpose of the funding will in large part determine the type of financial package which should be offered for sale. The potential providers will differ in their attitude to risk, the return which they seek and the form which their funding takes. In addition, some sources will specialise in particular industries or in types of company.

Below are listed the broad types of sources of permanent capital which might be available to the independent private company:

● business expansion scheme;
● venture capital funds;
● development capital funds;
● pension funds and insurance companies.

The form which a funding proposal might take is covered in Chapter 8.

Business expansion scheme (BES): At the time of writing, companies which are eligible for BES investment offer qualifying investors the prospect of income tax relief on the amount invested, subject to certain statutory restrictions, and freedom from capital gains tax on first sales of BES shares. As a result, to a 60% income tax payer the effective cost of say a £40,000 investment (the most allowed under the BES in any one year) could be as low as £16,000. This clearly improves the risk/reward ratio.

BES investment, which must all be in the form of ordinary shares, was designed to make it easier for entrepreneurs with good ideas and little capital to find risk funding. Typical investment propositions may include start-ups, young companies with little or no track record, small but expanding companies who need risk capital in order to fund further product research or market development, and perhaps management buy-outs.

The investment may come from friends or contacts established through the company's professional advisors at one end of the spectrum, to specific individual BES fund-raising exercises at the other. In between, specialist BES funds have been set up in order to spread investor risks further and thereby to make BES yet more attractive to the investor.

Pricing a BES issue is a matter of negotiation between the seller and the buyer. As with all investments in developing companies, the greater the potential and the more credibly it can be presented, the better the deal for the raiser of funds.

Venture capital funds: In the USA venture capital funds take a very sporting and almost speculative view of investments, very often providing funding for projects which are far removed from immediate exploitation. Many of these projects fail, but some succeed, and the rewards on those that succeed are huge.

In the United Kingdom there are few such pure venture capital funds. Instead, the English version of the venture capital fund tends to be a slightly riskier development capital fund with a specialisation in a particular industry. Therefore, the factors which feature in typical propositions and the investor perspectives tend to be the same as those for development capital (see below).

Development capital: As indicated above, the distinction between venture and development capital can become blurred. Pure development capital funds will look for established profitable companies which require funds for expansion, but which have no desire to obtain an immediate Stock Exchange quote.

Typically, sums of £100,000+ will be available, to be invested in the form of equity or a mixture of equity and loans. Typically, the development capital organisation will look for very specific features in any potential investment:

- a well-reasoned prospect of success;
- management competence;
- an adequate equity stake;
- board representation;
- a way of realising their investment.

However, in return (besides funds) many of them offer management support and for those with industry specialisations, access to useful contacts.

Once again, pricing a deal with a development capital fund is a matter of negotiation between the seller and the buyer.

Pension funds and insurance companies: Private placings with pension funds, insurance companies and other investing institutions can be a sensible alternative to other sources of funds.

Such investors are more interested in high immediate running yields than in eventual large capital gains, and are more concerned with the underlying financial stability of the investee than with voting control or equity rights. For that reason the usual course of action is to place preference shares with such investors.

The advantages to the investors are clear. The yield is fixed at above market average and ranks for payment before any returns are paid to the ordinary shareholders. The security in liquidation is also better than that afforded to the ordinary shareholders. The shareholders benefit in that the preference shares do not normally have any votes, and so there is no question of loss of control even in a substantial fund-raising exercise. Finally, the investee company benefits, since under normal circumstances the preference shares count as equity for purposes of assessing gearing ratios and borrowing capacity.

In its simplest form, this sort of deal is suitable only for established companies with predictable earnings and sound assets. Pricing of the deal will depend on market interest rates and the market yield on quoted preference shares. The amount which can be raised from this source will depend on the amount and quality of business assets, the degree of borrowing and the extent to which earnings cover preference dividends.

Raising permanent capital through a quotation

In this context quoted means public. Companies can go

public on a variety of public markets, each of which has different requirements:

- full listing on the Stock Exchange;
- quotation on the Unlisted Securities Market (USM);
- quotation on the Over-the Counter markets (OTC).

"Going public" in whatever market has many attractions. Besides providing the company with ready access to funds which have a relatively low cash cost, there is the prospect of realising some of the shareholders' wealth through the sale of shares into a public market, and the added prestige that being a public company brings. Against these advantages must be set the disadvantages of being subject to a continuous pressure to perform and pay dividends, and ceaseless scrutiny by financial journalists, stockbrokers and the general public.

Full listing on the Stock Exchange: In order to become a security fully listed on the Stock Exchange a company must undergo a full flotation. A flotation can take a number of different forms:

- *Offer for sale:* In this arrangement the Issuing House (a merchant bank or a stockbroker) buys the shares from the company to be floated at an agreed price. It then offers them on for sale to the public at a slightly higher price. The difference between the buying and selling price is the underwriting commission. The advantage to the company of this arrangement is that certainty of raising the desired funds is assured since the share issue is fully underwritten.

- *Prospectus issue:* In this form of flotation, which is rarely seen, there is no Issuing House involved, and the shares are not underwritten. Instead, the shares are offered to the public by the company. In this way the underwriting costs are avoided but there is a greater degree of risk of the flotation being a failure.

- *Placing of shares:* Often used on the Unlisted Securities Market, a placing involves selling the new shares to clients of the Issuing House directly. In that way the company being floated avoids most of the publicity and advertising costs associated with an offer for sale.

- *An introduction:* Introductions are uncommon, and involve an application for listing being made without any simultaneous arrangements to sell shares. The Stock Exchange will only permit such an arrangement when the ownership of the shares is already well dispersed.

Quotation on the Unlisted Securities Market (USM): The USM came into being in 1980 in order to provide a public market for the shares of smaller companies. It is similar in many ways to the traditional listed market, but there are less onerous requirements regarding the minimum size of the flotation, flotation costs and the level of supporting information which needs to be set out in the flotation documents. The methods of floating companies which can be used are similar to those available on the main market, and in most respects, once the company is established in the market there is little practical difference between a USM dealing facility and a full quote on the main market.

Quotation on the Over-the-Counter markets (OTC): There are a number of OTC markets run by specialist firms who either act as principals (ie hold stock in their own right) or match buyers and sellers. The main advantages of an OTC quotation is that it is better than no quotation at all, and that the disclosure of information requirements are much lower. However, an OTC quotation does not confer the same access to wide capital markets as either the USM or the main market, and may not provide a company with the fund-raising facilities it needs.

The pricing of shares for any of these public methods of fund raising is largely an art. We have seen accusations of misjudgement levied by the press and others at the most experienced of professional advisors, as witness Amersham International some time ago, and more recently, British Telecom and perhaps Wellcome.

Pricing is largely built up based on the relationship between the earnings and the share price of existing public companies which are similar to the company to be floated. A further discussion of company valuation can be found in Chapter 10.

5. Calculation of cost of capital

Chapter 10 will deal with the appraisal of long-term projects where, because of the duration and size of the project, the cost of funding becomes one of the most significant considerations affecting project viability. The basic principle to be applied in a number of appraisal techniques is that projects should be accepted if their rate of return exceeds the cost of capital to the organisation. Quite simply, the cost of capital needs to be accurately known since it is a critical ingredient in the financial assessment of whether or not projects should be proceeded with.

As we have seen earlier in this Chapter, different providers of funds acquire different risks in connection with their share of the funding of an operation. In summary:

Source	Type of funds	Degree of risk (to provider)	Cost of funds
Banks	Secured lending	Low	Base rate +1-3%
Institutions	Preference shares	Medium	Base rate +2-5%
Funds	Equity	High	High give away of equity and earnings
Stock market	Equity	Varies	Cash cost less than 4% where growth is likely but much higher where there is little chance of growth*

*But see below for further discussion of the cost of capital for such companies.

The taxation treatment of the costs of servicing these sources of funds differs and can have a significant bearing on the eventual net cost of funds to the business. In particular, it should be remembered that detailed rules may change from year to year. In the examples quoted below, corporation tax has been taken as 35% and the basic rates of income tax as 29%.

For most companies cost of capital has two components:

- the cost of debt;
- the cost of equity capital.

The cost of debt can be easily measured. It is simply the interest charged on funds borrowed. Interest charged on debt is deductible in arriving at the company's taxable profit, so that the net cost of this form of capital is reduced. For example, if the cost of borrowing were to be 10%, the effective after-tax cost (assuming that the company was making taxable profits) would be 7.5%.

The cost of equity capital is an implied cost. It is not a return that has to be paid to the shareholders; rather, it is a notional rate of return which has to be earned in order to ensure continued investment by the shareholders. That notional rate of return has two constituents:

- the real return paid to the shareholders, ie the dividend;
- the notional return attributable to the shareholders because of the growth of the company's net assets through profit retention, market sentiment etc.

The returns which have to be earned in the market-place for the shareholders in total might be defined as:

$$\text{current market price} \times \text{cost of capital}$$

Those returns are equal to the sum of:

$$\text{dividends} + (\text{current market price} \times \text{growth rate})$$

Or,

$$\text{Cost of capital} = \frac{\text{dividends}}{\text{current market price}} + \text{the growth rate}$$

This explains the fact that companies with little to offer in the way of growth prospects have to pay high dividends in relation to their share price. Conversely, companies with very good prospects have very low dividend yields.

The average cost of capital for a company is the combined weighted average of the cost of debt and of equity capital.

For example, a certain public company has the following capital structure:

Capital structure —

Debt	£41,000,000
Equity	£58,000,000
Total capital	£99,000,000

59

Cost —

Debt	13% before tax, or 8.45% after tax
Equity — dividends	1.33 pence per share
— anticipated growth	14% based on historic performance
— market price	35 pence

The average cost of capital (ie that rate of return which must be exceeded by any new project in order to improve the returns to shareholders) is:

Proportion of Capital		Cost of debt		Proportion of capital		Price yield		Dividend yield
$\frac{41}{99}$	$\times$	8.45	$+$	$\frac{58}{99}$	$\times$	$\left(14\right.$	$+$	$\left.\frac{1.33}{35}\right)$

which amounts to 13.93%.

It is immediately apparent that the cost of debt is less than the full cost of equity capital. However, we have already seen that the introduction of significant debt into a business introduces additional risks to the shareholders. Specifically, it increases the risk of fluctuations of earnings due to economic factors (interest rate changes) and it reduces the shareholders' claim on the most secure assets of the business.

Thus there is a difference of views on the benefit of borrowing, between the company, which is receiving funds, and the owners of that company:

Company	Shareholders
Generally, the average cost of capital reduces as debt content increases.	The perception of risk increases as the proportion of borrowings to total capital increases.

As a consequence, only an initial level of debt is likely to reduce the cost of capital. Thereafter, as the perceived risk increases, the shareholders will seek to add a risk premium to their returns. Hence cost of capital will rise. Thus levels of borrowing need to be carefully set to provide a controlled balance of benefits.

Chapter 4

The business as a system of costs and revenues

We have already seen that financial engineering embraces a great variety of different tasks. Those tasks might be summarised as follows:

- managing the financial aspects of the moving parts of a business — that is to say, the relationships between revenues and variable costs, and the levels of working capital which are needed to support day-to-day trade;
- managing the financial aspects of the fixed components of the business — the machines, plant, premises and other infrastructure items which have long lifetimes and which are exploited by the business over extended periods of time;
- designing the best funding structure to suit the needs of the business;
- planning the long and short-term future and anticipating problems and opportunities and forecasting their financial impact;
- installing financial controls so that transactions are appropriately recognised and reported, and that corrective action is taken if necessary.

Not many managers will have obvious day-to-day responsibility for all of these areas. Quite reasonably, they will regard their responsibilities within their business or business segments as a series of short and long-term operational tasks, which should lead to the desired results if executed correctly. Typically, those results may be expressed as market share, product quality, order/delivery relationship etc. All businesses have objectives in these areas; for some, objectives may be set as part of the corporate planning process; for others, they may simply reside unspoken in the minds of the owners.

However, all business decisions have financial implications. Whether it is recruiting extra labour, bringing out a new model, closing down a factory or taking on a new public relations agency, the action would not be contemplated unless the possibility of a financial benefit is foreseen, and there is probably also an associated cost. The job of the manager is to make the right business decisions and to achieve certain business aims and objectives. Consequently, he needs to know the likely financial impact of his decisions. His decisions need to make sense financially as well as operationally. In this way, every manager becomes a financial engineer.

This Chapter describes how to use a simple financial model of the profit and loss account to improve business decision-making. The model can be customised for any business, but the simple version described is based on the fundamental cost structure of any business. In summary, business costs are categorised according to behaviour, and the concepts thus developed can then be applied to business control and short-range planning.

The other aspects of financial engineering described above are covered in subsequent Chapters.

1. The nature of costs and revenues

For purposes of planning, estimating and reporting, costs need to be divided into groups which reflect the way they link into and change with business events.

In any business costs are incurred within two main behavioural categories:

- *Variable costs* are those costs which, in total, vary with the level of throughput.

  For example, for most manufactured products the cost of raw materials will increase or decrease in direct proportion to the number of units of product which are made. Payroll is sometimes considered to be a variable cost, but in many industries it is not, since the employer may have entered into a minimum guaranteed wage agreement or similar arrangement, or when it is simply not practicable to lay people off.

- *Fixed costs* are those costs which do not vary in total when throughput or activity levels change.

  For example, the costs of insurance, rates or administration personnel will not vary as throughput levels change in the factory. All of those costs are fixed indirect costs or fixed overheads. However, there are also some overheads which are not fixed. Those are items like power or scrap cost which cannot be allocated to specific units of production, but which do change with output.

Various cost behaviour patterns are demonstrated in the following examples:

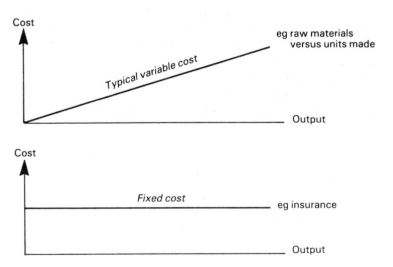

However, in practice not all costs behave in this simple and convenient fashion. The cost of employing people is significant in most industries, and is often a basic unavoidable fixed cost with an overlay of cost increments in steps as extra employees are recruited:

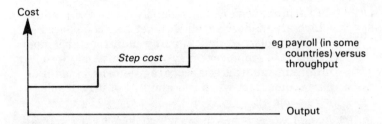

A further complication might be that the extra cost incurred to step up the output by recruiting extra manpower might be less than that saved by reducing manning levels in response to subsequent drops in output. Diagrammatically:

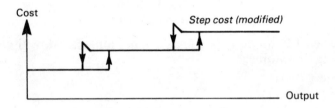

As output is reduced (to match market conditions), people are kept on beyond the point at which they were originally taken on. As output reduces further, redundancy payments are made in order to reduce the labour force.

Another common cost behaviour, similar to the above is the "standing charge plus usage":

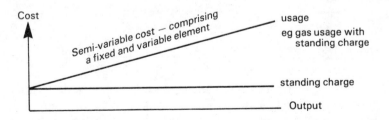

The business as a cost-generator

The total costs of a business can be drawn up in a diagrammatic summary as follows:

VARIABLE COSTS
raw materials
production wages

+

FIXED COSTS
administration
selling etc

=

TOTAL COSTS

In practice, this deceptively simple model allows for meaningful and useful analysis of business activity, particularly since it can be applied within a business to review the performance of different segments of that business.

On page 30 we saw that Intertrade Limited had some difficulty in establishing the precise cost of stocks. Let us continue with Intertrade Limited as an example. Intertrade manufactures and sells a range of quality soft toys. In addition, in order to ensure that a full range is offered to customers, it also merchandises a number of complementary lines of toys. Intertrade has a buying department which buys raw materials for own manufacture, a factory, a sales force (the sales director buys in all the toys manufactured outside), and an administration department.

The annual fixed costs of running these departments approximate —

Buying department	36,000
Factory	146,000
Sales force	110,000
Administration	50,000
	342,000

In 1985, Intertrade sold £500,000 of factored toys. Suppliers were paid £350,000 in respect of those toys. Sales of own manufactured toys amounted to £500,000, and the related raw materials and labour costs were £350,000. As a result, Intertrade made a loss of £42,000 in that year. The profit and loss account was as follows:

Sales	1,000,000
Cost of sales	700,000
Gross margin	300,000
Overheads	342,000
Net loss	(42,000)

It is clear that up to a certain point, the costs of each segment of Intertrade's business run independently. Thereafter, costs are shared, or incurred in a common pool. Furthermore, a basic unavoidable level of costs has been committed, whether Intertrade makes any sales or not. A certain amount of analysis needs to be done in order to discover where the losses occurred and what action ought to be taken.

The cost structure of Intertrade may be modelled thus:

Activity:	Manufacturing	Factoring
VARIABLE COSTS raw materials production wages	350,000	350,000

+

FIXED COSTS attributable to — factory buying	146,000 36,000	NIL
central overhead — administration selling	50,000 110,000	

=

TOTAL COSTS 1,042,000

Thus the independent element of the costs incurred by each business segment can be split into its variable and fixed cost constituents. It can then be compared with the revenues generated by that business segment. Thus for Intertrade:

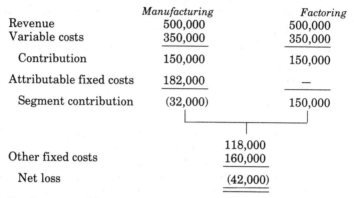

	Manufacturing	*Factoring*
Revenue	500,000	500,000
Variable costs	350,000	350,000
Contribution	150,000	150,000
Attributable fixed costs	182,000	—
Segment contribution	(32,000)	150,000
	118,000	
Other fixed costs	160,000	
Net loss	(42,000)	

In the case of Intertrade, the analysis shows that the manufacturing segment of the business is not earning its keep. In turn, that may be due to volume shortfalls, production inefficiencies, or overspending on fixed costs. Naturally, the outcome of such an analysis will lead to swift corrective action!

Many businesses do not have the information to conduct an analysis of this kind. In practice, the first steps which need to be taken may be to ensure that a proper distinction is drawn between those costs which are variable and those which are fixed.

2. Value added and contribution

Imagine that in the example above instead of the headings "Manufacturing" and "Factoring", the headings read "Clothing" and "Electronics"; or "Baking" and "Confectionery" or anything at all. The information presented to us would still tell us which segment was profitable, and the extent to which that segment's profit contributed towards paying for shared business infrastructure facilities.

The point is that to the financial engineer the product is

not of itself important. What is important is the way in which that product contributes profit and cash to the business. Therefore, if financial information is to be useful for making decisions, it must show by product or by appropriate business segment the volumes and sale prices achieved, and the relationship between those volumes and the associated variable costs.

The variable costs of most manufactured products consist of two principal ingredients:

- *Raw materials* — we have already seen the importance of raw materials as a basic variable cost. The basic requirement which raw materials have to fulfil in order to fall into this category is to have a definable and fixed value usage which remains constant per unit of output. As long as that is the case the total raw materials cost of production will vary directly in proportion to throughput.

- *Labour* — we have seen that labour may or may not be a variable cost. In many businesses labour costs are identifiable with units of output, but if activity drops below a minimum level, wages are guaranteed irrespective of whether the workforce is productive or not. Under such circumstances direct labour functions as a step or semi-variable cost (see graphs on page 64). Alternatively, in some businesses (such as the professions) certain classes of employee may not be paid overtime. In those cases, costs are fixed for smallish increases in activity, but increase in steps for larger-scale increments in output as new employees need to be taken on (see graph of step costs on page 64).

Thus, in order to be useful as an analytical tool in businesses where labour costs are not truly variable, the profit and loss account needs to set out separately true variable costs and semi-variable costs such as labour:

		Nature of costs
Revenues (ie sales)	X	
Direct costs — materials	(X)	variable
VALUE ADDED	XX	
Direct costs — labour	(X)	step
CONTRIBUTION	XX	
Fixed costs	(X)	fixed
Net profit	XX	

Value added is the wealth created internally within the enterprise. That wealth is then used to pay wages, to fund further investment, to pay taxation and to reward the owners of the enterprise. It is a useful concept, because the value added per unit of output can normally be calculated precisely, and usually remains fixed over the whole range of possible output volumes.

Contribution is defined as revenue less direct costs. Alternatively, it can be defined as the amount each unit of output sold pays towards the infrastructure of the business. It is an important concept because it can be used to determine and control the minimum viable level of activity for a business.

3. Breakeven

Most managerial decisions in relation to planning and control require a knowledge of the way costs behave in aggregate in response to changes in the level of activity. This enables profit levels to be estimated at different levels of output or capacity utilisation.

However, the most important piece of management information which needs to be known by all entrepreneurs is the minimum level of activity at which their business will survive. That level of activity is the breakeven point for that particular business at that particular time.

Breakeven analysis

Breakeven analysis is a technique which can be used to

assess the level of activity which needs to be achieved in order to ensure that all costs are covered.

In the previous section we saw that the amount each unit sold earns for the business, before fixed costs are considered, is termed contribution. At any level of activity, algebraically,

CONTRIBUTION = REVENUES − VARIABLE COSTS

At the point where the business is breaking even, contribution must equal fixed costs. Algebraically:

PROFIT = 0 = CONTRIBUTION − FIXED COSTS

or,

CONTRIBUTION = FIXED COSTS

This relationship is best illustrated by way of a diagram called a breakeven chart. The breakeven chart matches the contribution generated by a business enterprise with the fixed costs of that enterprise:

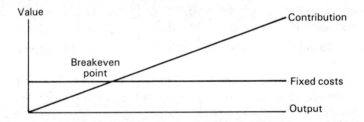

The usefulness of this technique becomes evident when we consider that costs (both fixed and variable) are relatively well known; however, revenues derived from marketing may not be. Breakeven calculations permit the financial engineer to calculate the sales or activity levels needed to breakeven, and then to ask the question:

"Are we likely to make the sales we need to breakeven?"

Using further the information analysed from Intertrade Limited's 1985 results (reproduced below):—

The business as a system of costs and revenues

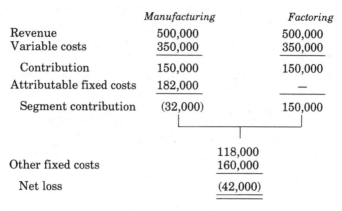

	Manufacturing	Factoring
Revenue	500,000	500,000
Variable costs	350,000	350,000
Contribution	150,000	150,000
Attributable fixed costs	182,000	–
Segment contribution	(32,000)	150,000
	118,000	
Other fixed costs	160,000	
Net loss	(42,000)	

Manufacturing of own toys will break even within its own segment if contribution can be increased by £32,000. That increase can come from improved volume as follows:—

$$\text{Contribution per £ sales} = \frac{150,000}{500,000} = .30$$

Extra contribution needed = 32,000

$$\text{Therefore extra sales required} = \frac{32,000}{.3} = £107,000 \text{ (approx).}$$

Because costs are generally known, it is quite feasible to insert the desired or minimum acceptable level of profit in the formula, and use known or expected fixed and variable costs to determine the required level of sales, or *volume target*.

In order to see how a volume target might be set using the breakeven concepts described above, consider a small businessman (Alan) thinking of setting up a hamburger stall outside a major all-year tourist attraction. Because there is no competition, he believes he can sell just one type of better-quality hamburger at a slight premium. Other relevant information is:

Company : Alan's Fastfoods Ltd.
Product : Hamburgers
Selling price : £2.00 per hamburger
Variable cost : Buns .7p+Burgers 38p+other 5p=50p
Fixed cost : Rent of pitch £2,000 per annum

Naturally, Alan wants to make a profit out of his

enterprise, and so wishes to assess in the first instance whether or not the venture will at least breakeven, and then whether it is likely to make sensible levels of profit.

The financial engineering questions he needs to answer are:

(i) How many hamburgers need to be sold per annum to breakeven? (And, does he think he can sell that many?)

(ii) How many hamburgers need to be sold per annum to earn £20,000? (And, does he think he can sell that many?)

Answer:

Required contribution = Fixed costs + Profit

= i) £2,000 + £0 = £2,000
= ii) £2,000 + £20,000 = £22,000

Volume targets:

Contribution = Revenue − Variable costs
= £2.00 − (.07 + .38 + .05)

The contribution per hamburger is £1.50

i) To breakeven, £2,000/1.5 (= 1,333) hamburgers must be sold.

ii) To make £20,000 a year, £22,000/1.5 (= 14,666) hamburgers must be sold (ie about 40 a day)

Breakeven analysis is a vital tool for the financial engineer. An example is given below for the reader to attempt. It illustrates a simple instance of how the technique may be applied in practice.

Albema Fish Trattoria —

Albema Fish Trattoria is a specialist high-quality restaurant famous throughout London for its fish dishes and the excellent quality and speed of its service. The owner, Giovanni Serlio, is considering expansion since he considers the restaurant to be successful as it is fully booked every night and he has to turn potential diners away.

The Albema is located in Covent Garden close to the underground station and near to the Royal Opera House and the theatres. The restaurant seats 80 people and has a total square footage floor area of 2,200 square feet. Besides Giovanni and his wife Mirabella, the staff establishment consists of seven waiters, two chefs and one general helper. Giovanni pays the waiters £5,000 apiece plus tips. There is a strong but low value lunchtime trade during weekdays which is essentially one sitting, with a much higher value evening business which roughly falls into the pattern of two sittings, one at 7:00 pm and one at 10:30 pm. This corresponds to the timing of theatre performances. The trade continues at about the same level all the year round — there is little, if any, seasonality.

Giovanni has the opportunity of renting a further 800 square feet of space suitable for conversion to restaurant use. This space is next to his existing premises, and could be served out of the existing kitchens. The extra space would allow him to seat a further 50 people. The extension and conversion work would cost £120,000, which would be funded by a five year loan. The rent and rates would amount to £12,000 annually. Furniture leasing would amount to £6,000 annually. Other fixed costs would approximate £24,000 annually.

Recent typical financial results for the Albema have been as follows (month of June):

	Covers	Value
Sales	6,080	106,880
Food and beverage costs		(74,630)
		32,250
Payroll		(9,200)
Rent and rates		(2,000)
Depreciation over 5 years		(9,050)
Other fixed costs		(7,000)
Net profit before tax		5,000

The general economic climate is good, although interest rates are high at 15%.

Advise Giovanni whether he should extend his premises or not, and what further investigations he should make before finally deciding whether or not to expand.

An answer is given below.

Albema Fish Trattoria — a possible solution

The two key questions are firstly, how many covers does

Giovanni need to attract to ensure that the restaurant extension pays for itself, and secondly, can he be sure that those covers will materialise if he goes ahead.

- How many covers does Giovanni need to attract to ensure that the restaurant extension pays for itself?

Good information is available about the extra fixed operating costs which will be incurred if the extension proceeds. The annual amounts of those costs are as follows:

Fixed costs:

Construction work, amortised over 5 years	24,000
Rent and rates	12,000
Lease of furniture	6,000
Other fixed costs	24,000
	66,000

Step costs:

There will also be a step cost incurred if more waiters are needed to serve the new area. Based on the square footage to be added and on the reputation of the existing restaurant for quality and speed of service it seems likely that at the absolute minimum, at least two further waiters will be needed. That will cost a further £10,000 per annum.

Financing costs:

In addition, there will be financing costs incurred on the money needed to fund the construction work. The full amount has to be borrowed, and the current cost will be 15% of £120,000, ie £18,000 per annum.

Thus total additional costs will amount to £94,000 per annum.

Information about future income and costs can only be obtained by extrapolating from past experience. Contribution (the net of revenue less variable costs) is directly proportional to covers served. Covers served in June (which was a typical month) averaged a contribution of £3.66 per cover.

If the total additional annual costs are £94,000, then the additional number of covers which need to be served annually are (94,000/3.66), which amounts to about an extra 70 per day.

- Can Giovanni be sure that 70 extra covers per day will materialise if he goes ahead?

The maximum capacity of the extension is 50 persons at three sittings a day, ie 150 covers per day. Therefore, the breakeven level is well within the capacity to be added. However, it is not known whether the likely level of covers which will be served is 10, 60 or 100. The only information available is that diners are being turned away.

Therefore, the correct answer to this situation is to ask Giovanni to survey and quantify the bookings which he is currently having to turn away, to see whether those bookings over some period indicate that the volume target of 70 is likely to be met.

This example shows the way in which known or extrapolated information can be used to project into uncertainty and to establish working targets. It also shows how financial success depends to some extent on management policies. The breakeven point would be lower if no extra waiters were required, but presumably standards of service would go down. Conversely, if service standards and the number of waiters were to be increased, the breakeven point would go up.

Other aspects

The time which must elapse between implementation of change and appearance of the results must be taken into account by the financial engineer. Many direct costs can be controlled on a day-to-day basis. Change horizons for indirect costs are usually much longer. As a result of this fundamental difference, separate methods need to be developed to control such costs and to evaluate decisions which may affect the different types of cost to differing degrees. In general:

- variable or operating costs are usually set out in an operational budget with a short time horizon;
- fixed costs associated with business infrastructure are usually derived from a capital budget with a much longer time perspective.

The absolute level of fixed versus variable costs in a business or in a project is important since it determines the committed risk inherent in the project. For example a contract cleaning operation involving non-union and part-time labour (all variable cost) would not require as much commitment as an investment in an hotel (which would substantially consist of fixed costs).

4. Breakeven and pricing

There are three important and different elements of information which need to be blended when designing selling prices:

- the minimum profit margin required;
- the cost of creating the product or service;
- the price which the market will bear.

The minimum profit margin required

This is perhaps the most neglected of the three elements, since it is often assumed that a project or product will be successful as long as it can make a profit. In fact, projects or products can earn profits but be miserable failures, because those profits are insufficient.

All businesses exist to earn a return on the capital put in by the owners. The rate of return that has to be earned will be determined by a great number of factors, the most important of which will be the funding requirement of the business and the rates of return earned by other investment opportunities which present themselves to the owners. These factors can and should be considered as part of the long-range planning process, which will be elaborated on in subsequent Chapters. In summary, the pricing process should build into the selling price sufficient margin to permit the product to fund its own working capital requirements as well as producing a rate of return acceptable to the investors.

The cost of creating the product or service

It seems obvious to say that the cost of providing a product or service should be known. However, often it is not. Instead, those costs are known which are uniquely related to the product or service. Other costs which are directly related to the product, but which may be used in a number of different products, can easily be mixed together and reported as a single cost.

Once again, direct costs may be defined as that expenditure which may easily be identified with a particular unit of output or with a particular section of the productive organisation. The direct costs of making a unit of furniture will include the wood, the ironmongery, any glass that may be used, and the cost of paying the people who have worked on the unit (including their national insurance contributions, holiday pay and benefits). Similarly, the direct costs of providing a service such as a 12,000 mile car service will be the costs of the parts renewed and the cost of paying the mechanic's wages.

In some businesses, direct costs may be a very small part of total costs. For example, a cruise liner or scheduled aircraft still makes its journey with all of its staff and with substantially the same fuel cost and landing dues irrespective of whether it is full or half full. Strict direct costs which vary with the number of passengers on board may consist only of the cost of consumables given away, such as food and drink.

Different pricing considerations apply to indirect costs, which are often termed overheads, and which can be defined as that expenditure which is needed in order to provide the business capacity of the enterprise.

Because indirect costs generally relate to the infrastructure of the business (ie factory capacity, administration personnel, insurance etc), they cannot be specifically linked to any particular unit of output. Those costs are often related to time (insurance, rates and administration salaries are good examples). The key to the correct pricing decision is knowledge of the level of capacity at which the infrastructure is operating. If it is running at below full capacity, then selling prices which are above direct cost (ie which make a contribution) are worthwhile.

When pricing, it is worth remembering that because of their direct link with production or level of activity, the response of most direct costs to controlling action is rapid.

However, because of the longer-term nature of indirect costs, many of them can only be controlled over the longer term.

The price which the market will bear

Sales or marketing managers would probably say that in most markets prices must be set in comparison with direct or indirect competitors. (Direct competitors for a biscuit manufacturer might be other biscuit manufacturers; indirect competitors might be cake manufacturers). However, from a financial engineer's perspective that statement is in itself insufficient.

The fact is that in an ideal world price could be managed so as to ensure the greatest level of financial return. And the greatest level of financial return is earned when the sum of the contributions (selling price less variable cost) of the various customers and products is greatest. In turn, the sum of all the contributions is derived from the contribution of each individual transaction and the volume of those transactions.

Contribution levels are subject to two constraints — market forces on the selling price and the direct cost of the product. Volume is also subject to two constraints — market demand and ability to supply.

In other words, pricing into a market should depend on the ability of the business to make a profit from sales into that market, rather than on the ability of the business to sell to that market. That, in turn, depends on the total operating capability of the business, and the current level of usage of its resources.

Pricing for profit

The simple diagram of the business as a cost generator can be modified to show the business as a generator of profits, as follows —

```
┌─────────────────────────┐
│       REVENUES          │
│          −              │
│    VARIABLE COSTS       │
│          =              │
│     CONTRIBUTION        │
└─────────────────────────┘
            −
┌─────────────────────────┐
│      FIXED COSTS        │
│     administration      │
│       selling etc       │
└─────────────────────────┘
            =
┌─────────────────────────┐
│        PROFITS          │
└─────────────────────────┘
```

The model illustrates that the following profit objectives must be addressed in any pricing decision:

- the aggregate contribution achieved must equal the fixed costs plus an adequate return for the shareholders;

- if the business is constrained by insufficient demand from the market-place, then any deal which provides a contribution to fixed costs should be considered (ie volume should be maximised, but at selling prices above variable cost);

- if the business is constrained by an inability to supply, then if feasible, short-term demand should be managed down by increasing selling prices (ie contribution should be maximised whilst maintaining full throughput). In the long-term, consideration should be given to expansion!

Let us consider some examples:

Adequacy of profit —

The situation:

Ximplex Limited has been doing very well recently. Sales have been growing at 25% compound per annum, and seem set to do so for the foreseeable future. Volumes sold last year were 12,000 units. Ximplex Ltd sells one particular advanced type of power supply unit. The sales price is always £25.00 per unit, and the variable costs (which are not expected to increase) are

79

£15.00. Fixed overheads run at £10,000 per month. One of the difficulties which the company has discovered to accompany their growth is that there is also growth in debtors and stocks, and the net investment required in working capital is growing at about 25% per annum. The net working capital last year was £100,000, fixed assets amounted to £300,000, and there are no borrowings.

Ximplex Limited is in the process of setting prices for the coming year. What financial considerations should be built into that process? (Ignore taxation).

The financial considerations:

Contribution required = fixed overheads + adequate profit.

Adequate profit = worthwhile return on funds provided by shareholders + sufficient profit to fund business growth.

Fixed overhead = £10,000 × 12 = £120,000

Worthwhile return on funds will be determined by the shareholders, but might be set at a commercial "interest" rate based on the net assets used in the business. In this case, the net assets used are £400,000, comprising fixed assets of £300,000 + net working capital of £100,000. A worthwhile return to be remitted out of the business might be 10%. Therefore, on this basis, profits of £40,000 are required.

To the returns required by shareholders must be added the funding need of the business. That increases in proportion to the increase in sales. Thus if net working capital was £100,000 last year, the current year requirement will be £100,000 + 25% or £125,000. The funding requirement is £25,000, which is best found from profits.

Fixed overheads + adequate profit
= Contribution required
= £120,000 + (£40,000 + £25,000) = £185,000

Contribution earned historically
= Sales price of £25 − variable cost of £15
= £10 per unit

Volume to be sold at a contribution level of £10 per unit in order to achieve required profit (ie *volume target*) = £185,000/£10 = 18,500 units.

But the probable volume to be sold, based on historical performance, is likely to be 25% up on the 12,000 units sold last year, ie 15,000 units. Therefore, there will be a sales shortfall of 3,500 units resulting in a profit shortfall of £35,000. What can be done?

Action to be taken will depend on commercial considerations:

If price increases are feasible without loss of volume, then a price increase per unit of £35,000 (the profit shortfall) divided by 15,000 (the number of units which will be sold), ie £2.33, will provide the required bottom line.

If price increases are not feasible, then perhaps volume can be increased by enhancing sales effort by recruiting an extra salesman. If the new salesman costs the business £20,000 a year, then he will have to sell 2,000 units (his fixed costs of £20,000 divided by the contribution of £10 per unit) in order to pay for himself. He also has to sell the volume shortfall of 3,500 units which was previously identified. Thus his target will be to sell 5,500 units. Can he do that?

Other potential courses of action can be costed in similar fashion.

Sales volume constraints

Ximplex Limited is constrained by volume of sales. Extra production can easily be accommodated without incurring extra fixed costs. Ximplex may take action to extend market share, along the fairly routine lines outlined above. However, in the hunt for new business it may be presented with opportunities to quote for substantial new orders at prices which, if the orders are to have any hope of being secured, have to be very low. The financial question which immediately arises is what is the minimum price acceptable to Ximplex which that company can quote.

Before responding to any such enquiry, it is important to remember that we are interested in contribution, that is, we wish to maximise sales revenues minus variable costs. In sales negotiations, all sorts of concessions can increase our variable costs. Extension of credit terms, improved warranty conditions and more frequent deliveries can all affect our costings, and therefore our estimates of negotiated contributions. Their impact should be quantified, and our normal contribution level amended accordingly.

In the case of Ximplex Limited, there are two deals available. Marsh & Co would like a quote for 3,000 units with no special arrangements, a call-off to suit our production schedules and will pay within 10 days of despatch. However, price is a major factor and the contract is out for tender. ARI Ltd want a tender for 4,500 units with a special packaging requirement costing £1 per unit and delivery dates are for mutual agreement. The units are for export, and therefore they require 120 days credit.

Marsh & Co

The standard variable cost of producing each unit (£15) is unchanged, consequently the price to be quoted should be as much as the market will bear, with the minimum breakeven price being £15,000. However, at a level of £15.00 per unit Ximplex is creating work for no benefit to itself, and therefore a normal acceptable minimum quote might be £17. At that level the contribution is £2 per unit (sales price of £17 less cost of £15), and the total contribution to profit is £2×3,000, ie £6,000. The increase in working capital levels is immaterial and therefore extra financing costs are minimal.

ARI Ltd

The standard variable cost of £15 is increased to £16 by the variable cost of packaging (£1). In addition, there is an additional variable cost with regard to finance, which relates solely to this potential contract. That amount is the interest cost of borrowing the money over the 120 day period to enable the contracted units to be made. At an interest rate of 15%, that amounts per unit to £16×.15 for 120 days, ie £0.79. Thus the variable cost is effectively £16.79 and that is also the breakeven price. However, once again at that level the company is creating work for no benefit, and therefore a normal acceptable minimum quote might be £19. At that level the contribution is £2.21 per unit (sales price of £19 less cost of £16.79), and the total contribution to profit is £2.21×4,500, ie £9,945.

Both of these opportunities offer the prospect of profitably overcoming the current sales volume constraints.

Capacity constraints

Ximplex Limited has so far come up with a range of possible actions to help it meet profitability targets. These might be summarised as follows:

	Units	Contribution
Probable sales — as is	15,000	£150,000
Marsh & Co tender	3,000	6,000+
ARI Ltd tender	4,500	9,945+
New salesman	5,500	35,000
	28,000	200,945+
Fixed costs		120,000
Net profit		80,945+

This profit is better than originally stipulated, but unfortunately Ximplex Limited cannot manufacture more than 25,000 units in its factory. It is therefore no longer likely to be constrained by market volumes, but instead is limited by ability to produce. What should it do?

Where demand exceeds supply, some of the demand has to be turned away. Demand can be turned away through outright rejection of business, or through imposition of business terms or conditions which are not acceptable to the customer. In this instance, Ximplex Ltd could decide to tender for the Marsh or ARI business at full price, knowing that if the work did come to them they would be earning enough out of it to warrant overtime working or special sub-contract arrangements. Alternatively, the company could decide to increase its prices across the board, in order to reduce demand and thus match it to capacity.

Applying financial engineering

With all of these financial figures flying around one might have forgotten the basic simplicity of the model. Here is is again:

```
┌─────────────────────────┐
│        REVENUES         │
│           −             │
│     VARIABLE COSTS      │
│           =             │
│      Selling price      │
│     × volume ×          │
│      gross margin       │
│           =             │
│      CONTRIBUTION       │
└─────────────────────────┘

             −

┌─────────────────────────┐
│      FIXED COSTS        │
│      administration     │
│       selling etc       │
└─────────────────────────┘

             =

┌─────────────────────────┐
│        PROFITS          │
└─────────────────────────┘
```

The examples have illustrated how the model works in practice, and have shown the relationship between four key business variables:

- fixed overheads;
- selling price;
- sales volume;
- contribution (or gross margin %).

A change in the relationships may be good or bad for the business, and the model allows us to simulate the effects of any change and discover what the impact might be. Sometimes, the effects are surprising.

> To continue with Ximplex Ltd, and model what might happen if that company increases selling prices not by £2.33, as suggested previously, but substantially, by £5.00. Under those conditions management believe that 20% of the existing business will be lost, and as a result, the volume of units sold will go down to 10,000. However, the margin, and hence the contribution on the residual sales will be much improved —

Selling price	£25	£30	£30
Volume	12,000	10,000	8,000
Gross margin	40%	50%	50%
Contribution	£120,000	£150,000	£120,000

In fact, the increase in prices is beneficial providing the volume does not reduce by more than a third, and with the expected volume drop, profits are improved by £30,000. For most businesses, along with the reduction in volume and the improved profits, will come an easing of the cash position due to a reduction of the net investment in working capital, and an improvement in customer relations, since the customers who depart at such times are generally the ones who are troublesome.

Fixed costs and risk

The greater the level of fixed costs in a business, the greater is the risk factor inherent in that business. The reason is evident from the model — fixed costs have to be paid out monthly (or weekly), whether or not there are any earnings, whereas variable costs are reduced when sales slump.

Once production limits are reached, the capacity provided by the business's fixed costs is exhausted. If capacity is expanded, fixed costs will increase as well. A management strategy to increase volume by reducing prices may prove to be disastrous if it is not correctly designed from a financial viewpoint. Such a policy may generate increased volume, lower profits, and a need to spend large sums quickly on unwarranted expansion.

Consider Ximplex's long-range ambitions to increase volume fourfold to 48,000 units per annum by dropping prices from the current £25.00 per unit to £20.00 per unit. That reduction of 20% in sales price corresponds to a reduction of 50% in the contribution per unit sold — from £10.00 to £5.00. The increase in volume means that a new production facility has to be built. That facility will add fixed costs of £120,000 to the existing fixed costs. The financial viewpoint is as follows:

	Current	*Proposed*
Volume	12,000	48,000
Sales price	25.00	20.00
Sales	300,000	960,000
Gross margin	40%	25%
Contribution	120,000	240,000
Fixed costs	120,000	240,000
Profit (loss)	–	–

The whole exercise introduces committed fixed costs without any assurance that sales levels will be achieved and without any prospect of profit even if sales levels are achieved.

In general, any business should seek to minimise its level of committed fixed costs, since by doing so, it reduces its vulnerability to unexpected setbacks.

Other mistakes

Other mistakes which can normally be anticipated and avoided by considering the business as a system of costs and revenues usually fall into two categories:

- costing mistakes, which are attributable to a lack of knowledge of the variable costs of manufacture or supply;
- structural mistakes, which are due to a failure to distinguish fixed costs attributable to an operating segment of the business from organisation-wide fixed costs.

Costing mistakes

There must be an infinite number of examples of costing mistakes, for example:

- failure to provide cover for the effect of exchange rate fluctuations on the price of raw materials which are imported from abroad,
- quotes for high specification work which do not take account of the attendant higher reject and scrap rate;
- power treated as a fixed cost when it is not;

- omission of related finance costs;
- disruption to existing established production.

The key to avoiding such mistakes is to research the quality and purpose of the information used to prepare quotations, assessments and proposals, and to pinpoint risk factors. If it is historical information, is it still valid? Has it been extracted on a consistent basis? And so on. An accountant's evaluation of a quote will be a dry weighing of data. A financial engineer will search for and recognise the weaknesses in that data and the risks in doing the business, and will cover them in some acceptable, commercial way, or will not do the business.

Structural mistakes

Structural mistakes usually arise from a poor managerial structure and a consequent poor recognition of cost generators.

Consider the example of Halo Manufacturers Limited. HML manufacture 3 different products on three different sites in the United Kingdom. As is usual in such cases, head office is located at the largest site, which is in the South-East (£000s):

Location	Product	Turnover	Profit (loss)
Site 1	Dynamos	5,000	200
Site 2	Motorised valves	8,000	200
Site 3	Pottery	4,000	(100)
Total group		17,000	300

Should Site 3 be closed or sold off, with a resultant enhancement of profitability?

The answer is that there is insufficient information to respond to that question. Specifically, we need to know how central (head office) costs affect reported profitability, and whether central costs would be reduced if Site 3 were to be closed. If we look again at the profit and loss structure with central costs in mind (£000s):

Location	Product	Profit before central costs	Central costs	Profit (loss)
Site 1	Dynamos	700	500	200
Site 2	Motorised valves	1,000	800	200
Site 3	Pottery	300	400	(100)
	Total group	2,000	1,700	300

In this instance, central costs are allocated across all three sites based on turnover. If central costs cannot be saved by the closure of Site 3 (which may well be the case), the effect of closure or sale would be (£000s):

Location	Product	Profit before central costs	Central costs	Profit (loss)
Site 1	Dynamos	700	654	46
Site 2	Motorised valves	1,000	1,046	(46)
	Total group	1,700	1,700	0

In other words, the closure or sale has eliminated the contribution that site made towards the fixed central costs of the organisation.

Mistakes of this kind have been made by big organisations. The key to avoiding them is to organise the enterprise's internal reporting in a way which reflects the nature and origin of costs.

Chapter 5

Managing business assets: working capital

Business organizations have to make investments in order to achieve their corporate objectives. Those investments are typically in land, buildings, plant, machinery, stocks of various types, debtors and cash. Their value and amount is set out in the balance sheet of that business.

In Chapter 2 we divided business assets into two financial categories:

- items which are continually transformed and renewed as part of the normal transaction cycle of the business. Those items include stocks, debtors and working cash balances net of creditors. At any point in time, the capital investment which is necessarily incurred in order to hold working levels of those items is the working capital requirement of that business;

- items which are purchased in order to create the capacity for the business to carry on its trade. Those items include plant, buildings, factory and office fixtures and fittings, computers, vehicles and similar long-lived assets. The cost of those items constitutes the infrastructure cost of the business.

Typically, working capital items are bought (or are created) in quantity and are held for short periods of time, whereas infrastructure assets are bought infrequently, usually as one-off purchases and have a lengthy business life.

Because of these very different attributes, the financial

management of business assets must be approached from two different directions:

- the effective management of working capital involves the striking of an acceptable balance between liquidity and profitability. In other words, control needs to be exercised over the short-term leads and lags in the transaction cycle, and over the absolute level of investment in working capital assets. For example, a very high level of stock may enable all orders to be met instantly, but will generally be very expensive to maintain because of high interest and storage costs;

- management of the business infrastructure is rather more difficult since it consists predominantly of assessing the probable benefits and costs of adding future business capacity of one sort or another. Furthermore, when organizations are assessing specific investment projects, they need to take account not only of the costs of the direct investment in the extra infrastructure needs of the project but also of the costs related to the extra working capital needs of that project. For example, the opening of a new retail showroom will not only entail the acquisition of premises (with the attendant cost commitments) but will also increase the amount of stock which needs to be carried. The extra cost of carrying that stock, which will primarily consist of interest charges, should be included in any financial feasibility assessment. Further complications arise when the investment to be made involves the development and marketing of new products which in some way are similar to those which currently exist. Those new products may replace or compete with the existing products (as, for example, the introduction of the motor car reduced the demand for rail travel, or the opening by a national chain of a new retail store in Derby may pull sales away from their existing store in Nottingham). The appraisal process needs to consider not only the direct effects of proceeding with the project under review, but also these "shadow" effects.

Management of working capital will be covered in this Chapter. Management of infrastructure investment will be covered in the next Chapter.

1. Working capital

Stocks and debtors are vital and unavoidable steps in the transaction chain for most businesses, yet they tie up costly funds. In addition, they limit room for growth and expansion, since few businesses have access to unlimited sources of finance. Thus a primary constraint which is likely to affect all businesses is the availability and the cost of funds required to finance the working capital.

Furthermore, the very fact that a business owns stocks and debtors in its own right exposes it to losses. Customers can become insolvent and unable to pay their debts, and stocks can deteriorate physically or become obsolete due to changes in fashion or technology.

For these reasons, enterprises should always seek to minimize the levels of working capital assets.

However, as levels of working capital assets are reduced, new constraints come into play and other costs may be incurred. Sales (and therefore contribution) can be lost either by an unwillingness to grant credit or by an inability to supply within the delivery schedules required by the customer. Suppliers may refuse to provide goods if the credit which they grant is over-extended. The workforce may stand idle if there is insufficient supply of raw materials or a shortage of components. Thus the costs of holding working capital assets need to be balanced against the income which may be lost by not holding them.

The amount of working capital which might be needed by an enterprise is determined by two factors:

- the time-lags inherent in the transaction cycle of the business;
- the volume of trade.

Time lags

The effect of time lags on the working capital requirement of a business can be broadly determined from a generalised model based on the fundamental transaction cycle:

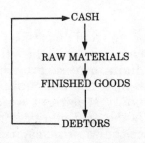

Time lags

C time taken to pay creditors from time of arrival of goods

R time taken to put goods into production from time of their arrival

P time taken to make product

F time product held in stock before sale

D debtor collection period

Under the terms and definitions used in this model, the total time taken for raw material to be physically turned into product and for the product to be sold is R + P + F. In money terms, further time delay is introduced by the need to provide credit (D), but this is mitigated by the credit provided by suppliers (C). The total time lag is:

$$(R + P + F) + (D - C)$$

or Processing time + credit term differential

The result of the above calculation gives the theoretical number of days during which the business has to fund its stock. That number of days, when multiplied by the value of average daily stock purchases gives the approximate working capital requirement of the business (see below— Volume effects).

> For example, in the case of Marks & Spencer plc, 1985 published accounts show that cost of sales was £2,293 million. Thus, the average daily purchase of materials was £6.28 million. Trade debtors were insignificant ("D" as defined above), and trade creditors amounted to £115 million, representing 18.3 days worth of purchases ("C" as defined above).

> Year-end stocks amounted to £230 million, which approximated to 36.6 days of sales ("R+P+F" as defined above). Consequently, R+C+F+D−C = 36.6+ 0−18.3 = 18.3, and the business was funding about 18.3 days worth of stock from its own resources.

The figure of 18.3 days calculated above is in itself meaningless. However, it acquires meaning when it is compared with other enterprises which are in the same line of business, or with the activities of the same business in earlier or later periods. Thus it can serve as an overall broad control over business performance in this area.

> Taking again the example of Marks & Spencer plc, we saw above that their suppliers were effectively funding half their stock. On the same basis, in the case of the 1985 accounts of J Sainsbury plc, the stock represented about 23 days sales and suppliers provided about 35 days credit. Thus suppliers were funding about one-and-a-half times the stockholding! Should Marks & Spencer use their undoubted strength to lever more credit from their suppliers?

Alternatively, the statistic can be used internally within business enterprises to assess the degree of efficiency with which working capital is managed.

> Again, consider Marks & Spencer. We have calculated the stockholding to be about 37 days. Could that figure be improved (ie reduced) without impairing the business? How much of that 37 days represented stock actually on the sales floor, where it was capable of being sold, and how much represented stock held in warehouses or in transit? Could the latter "idle time" be reduced?

You might want to calculate the "theoretical" transaction time-lags of your business. For example, if in theory suppliers give you 45 days credit ("C"), you in theory grant customers 30 days in which to pay ("D") and the full production cycle ("R+P+F") ought to be 15 days, you should have a net time-lag of zero. Compare that to what actually happens. How much credit do you actually take from your suppliers? How much credit do you really grant to your customers? How long does it actually take for stock to cycle through the factory (or shop) from receipt through to sale? The results of such a comparison may indicate areas for improvement!

Volume effects

The overall working capital requirement is:

time-lag × evaluated volume per day

If the cost of the stock is essentially accounted for by raw materials (ie labour and overheads are small), then the funding requirement of a business is the average daily purchase of raw materials multiplied by the number of days during which the business funds that stock. Alternatively, if a "safe" estimate is required, the funding need can be regarded as the sales per day multiplied by the time-lag. (This estimate is likely to be on the high side, since it includes the profit element of sales, which does not need funding.)

In any event, provided that there is a time-lag, there will always be an increased requirement for funds as the volume of business grows. This increased requirement can lead to the phenomenon known as over-trading. Over-trading occurs when a business expands volume to a level at which the ability of the business to provide working capital funding is exhausted. It does not matter that the trade may be profitable. The sheer volume cannot be sustained because the bank quite simply will not allow more credit. For example:

> Elixir of Life Limited is a pharmaceutical company specialising in natural herbal remedies. It exclusively supplies large retail outlets, and the market for its products has recently grown at a tremendous pace. The profit and loss results for the last two years' trading are given below together with the projected result for the current years (£000s):

	1984	1985	1986
Sales	1,100	2,350	3,980
Cost of sales	(737)	(1,705)	(3,156)
Gross margin	363	645	824
Other expenses	(312)	(482)	(603)
Pre-tax profit	51	163	221
Taxation	(20)	(64)	(88)
	31	99	133

> The results show good sales growth and increases in pre-tax profit. But these positive features mask a significant decline in gross margins, and the effect of this expansion on the balance-sheet has yet to be considered.

> The company supplies large retail outlets, most of

which are substantial supermarket chains. They take between 80 and 100 days to pay (on average, 90 days). Suppliers to the company grant 30 days credit, but in practice the company takes about 45 days on average to pay them. The production cycle is about 30 days. Labour and overhead costs are insignificant, since the main element of cost of sales is the cost of the raw materials.

The time-lags in the transaction cycle are as follows:

	days
Debtors − creditors = 90 − 45 =	45
Production =	30
Net time-lag	75

This time lag has effectively remained constant as the company has grown. However, at the same time the volumes which need to be financed have increased significantly. The balance-sheets of the company at the different year-ends are shown below from the point of view of the owner of the business, and the point of view of the bankers to the business (£000):

The owner's view:

	1984	1985	1986
Fixed assets	300	350	400
Stocks	70	142	263
Debtors	275	587	995
Cash	0	0	0
	345	729	1,258
Creditors	(104)	(213)	(393)
Taxation	(20)	(64)	(88)
Bank overdraft	(105)	(317)	(589)
	(229)	(594)	(1,070)
Net current assets	116	135	188
Long-term debts	(120)	(90)	(60)
Net assets	296	395	528

The bank's view:

	1984	1985	1986
Bank borrowings (i)	225	407	649
Net assets (ii)	296	395	528
Ratio (i) : (ii)	.76	1.03	1.23

Clearly, as a proportion of the total funds provided, the

bank is becoming a disproportionately greater provider each year. That is because the financing requirement of this business is not being met by its profits. In the short term, the funding shortfall can probably be met by increased borrowings. However, unless the time-lags are reduced or margins are improved, sooner or later the borrowing capacity of the business (as determined by its bankers) will become exhausted, with dire consequences.

2. Management of stocks

The management of stock requires the identification and balancing of two different kinds of costs:

- Costs of holding stocks. These are generally tangible costs which increase as the level of stocks increases.
- Costs associated with holding zero or low levels of stocks. These are generally intangible or invisible costs which relate to profits foregone rather than to expenses incurred. For example, as stock levels are reduced the risk increases of sales being lost due to stockouts or production stoppages due to shortage of materials. Such costs could be substantially eliminated by holding larger amounts of stock. These costs tend to reduce as the level of stocks increases.

Costs of holding stocks

These costs tend to be fairly easily identifiable and include the following:

- *Financing costs*
  These are the costs of acquiring or providing funds to buy or create the stocks held. They broadly approximate the value of the stocks held multiplied by the cost of capital.

- *Storage costs*
  These are the costs of physically accommodating the stocks. These costs include such items as the rent of the storage space and the salaries of personnel employed in stock supervision and control. In the case of perishable stocks such as food, storage costs may well include such items as refrigeration.

● *Insurance cost*
This is the cost of insuring the stocks against loss from theft, damage, etc. For particularly valuable stocks, security guards may also have to be employed. A further cost might be losses actually incurred through theft, damage, etc, if not covered by insurance.

● *Obsolescence cost*
In many industries there is a substantial risk that if stocks are held for too long they may go out of fashion, or design specifications may change. Clearly, if that happens, those stocks will be difficult or impossible to sell, and will lose much of their original value. The longer that stocks are held, the greater the risks involved.

Stockholding costs can be considerable, and have been estimated to range from 20% to 100% or more per annum of the value of the stocks concerned. Costs will vary for each business, depending on the industry sector and the nature of the stocks concerned. For example, perishable stock (such as frozen prawns or fine bone china) which is particularly susceptible to theft or damage is likely to have a much higher carrying cost than non-perishable inventory such as builder's sand.

Costs of holding low (or zero) stocks

These costs tend to be rather less obvious, and the identification of actual amounts involved is difficult. Such costs include the following:

● *Cost of loss of customer goodwill*
If an organization is unable to supply its customers as and when they require supplies, it is likely to experience a loss of customer goodwill, with a subsequent damaging effect upon sales. The lower the stockholding level, the higher the probability of such costs being incurred. The extent to which a loss of goodwill actually occurs is likely to depend upon the market status of the organization. For example, a monopoly supplier may not suffer any effective loss of goodwill as a result of keeping customers waiting.

● *Ordering costs*
This relates to the cost of placing each order with a supplier, and includes associated costs such as the handling of the goods when delivered. The higher the number of orders, the greater the costs will be. Since low stock levels will normally be associated with frequent replacement ordering, they are more likely to be associated with greater ordering costs than high stock levels. Another important factor is that orders for large quantities are frequently associated with bulk discounts, allowing further savings.

Optimal inventory levels

In spite of the considerable difficulties involved in calculating the various costs referred to above, all businesses should strive to maintain the stockholding level which achieves the minimum total cost.

Control techniques designed to help optimise stock levels include:

● monitoring of global inventory turn or stock usage, which controls the overall level of stock (and thus controls the related cost of funding that stock);

● designating economic order quantities which provide the optimal balance of ordering costs against stock-holding costs;

● establishing buffer or safety stock levels, which allow for re-order lead times and which trigger re-orders at the latest appropriate time;

● establishing stock-out controls, which control the frequency of stock-outs and their impact, and thus measure the effect of low stockholding policies on customers.

Inventory turn monitoring

Stock turn is a global measure which permits a quick (albeit rough) assessment of stock levels (and therefore stockholding costs) in relation to the performance of the business. It compares the current stock value with the annual level of throughput. Stock turn may be defined as:

$$\frac{\text{Cost of sales}}{\text{Balance-sheet stocks}}$$

Alternatively, the number of days it will take to sell the current stock value can be used to measure stock performance. In that case, the definition is:

$$\frac{\text{Balance-sheet stocks}}{\text{Cost of sales}} \times 365$$

The relationships between the costs of holding stock and costs of not holding stock may be shown graphically as follows:

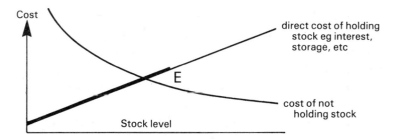

The aggregate costs are at their lowest at point E. This is the optimal level from a purely financial point of view. In practice, the appropriate level is difficult to determine since non-financial factors such as security of supply also play an important role. In many cases an empirical approach has to be adopted (but see below for further theoretical considerations).

Empirical techniques can include obtaining a global control figure from stock-turn monitoring which may be compared with the theoretical or ideal length of the production cycle. Alternatively, stock turn figures can be calculated by product segment or product line, to identify slow-moving or over-stocked items, or balanced against stock-out reports to determine whether stockholding policies are sound and are being successfully applied.

Determining economic order quantities

One particular problem with setting the optimal stock

level is that it will not be possible to maintain the exact stockholding level desired unless stock is replaced immediately it is used. In theory, the stockholding profile for a particular stocked item should steadily fall to zero and should then be immediately replaced by a further amount of stock. The new stock level, in turn, should steadily drop to zero to be once again replaced. In practice, it is likely that stocks will be used at a steady rate throughout the year but will be replaced in large block re-orders or production runs.

Once this process is recognised, it becomes apparent that there is a judgement to be made regarding the size of the re-order blocks. On the one hand, if re-ordering is done frequently in small quantities, stock levels can be kept low with a consequent saving of stockholding costs. On the other hand, as stock levels are reduced, the economies gained by holding stock are to some extent countered by the costs of frequent re-ordering, discounts foregone and similar expenses. At some point the aggregate of these costs is at a minimum, and the question arises—what is the most economic order quantity for inventory?

The economic order quantity can be calculated algebraically as follows:

> If: e is the order quantity,
> C is the cost associated with placing each order,
> A is the annual demand for (or usage of) the inventory item,
> H is the cost of holding one unit of inventory for one year.

Then we need to find the economic order quantity (E) at which the cost of carrying stock is equal to the cost of re-ordering that stock.

(i) Cost of carrying stock = Average stock level × cost per unit

$$= \frac{1}{2} \times e \times H$$

(ii) Cost of re-ordering stock = Number of re-orders × cost

$$= \frac{A}{e} \times C$$

At the minimum point, (i) and (ii) are equal, and the order quantity (e) is the economic order quantity (E).

$$E^2 = \frac{2AC}{H} \quad \text{or} \quad E = \sqrt{\frac{2AC}{H}}$$

This simple model has a number of weaknesses:

- Demand for the stock may fluctuate on a seasonal basis, in which case the straight averaging approach used may be substantially inaccurate.
- The annual demand can never be predicted with certainty, although statistical probabilities may be ascribed to various possible annual demands.
- The cost of loss of customer goodwill is not taken into account, ie the risk of running out of stock before the next delivery is ignored. If stock levels are very much fine-tuned to minimum levels, there is always a real risk that deliveries from suppliers may be delayed, causing a stock-out.

Establishing buffer or safety stocks

In theory, orders for stocks should be placed so that usage during the period up to delivery reduces stockholding to zero by the delivery date. However, because delivery lead times vary and demand for stock fluctuates, most organizations hold stocks which are above the minimum level. This excess stockholding is termed a buffer stock. The depth of the buffer stock which needs to be held should take into account:

- acceptable customer service levels;
- reliability of delivery scheduling by suppliers;
- predictability of demand;
- distribution and warehousing policy.

These factors can be addressed through statistical analysis or computer-based simulation and sensitivity analysis techniques.

Stock-out controls

One way of providing a check on the efficacy of stocking

policies (and of ensuring that stockholding reductions are not excessive) is to monitor the number of stock-outs and the time delay which they cause in completing orders. Some stock-outs are inevitable, but as always, it is a matter of striking the right balance between the costs of holding stock and the number and length of delays which are imposed on customers.

For manufacturing or distributive industries, the commercial balance which must be struck is:

> Desired customer service level (measured in terms of unfilled orders as a proportion of total orders received, or in terms of ageing of order backlog)
>
> *Versus*
>
> Costs of holding stocks

For service or capacity sale industries:

> Business turned away (measured by reference to income foregone)
>
> *versus*
>
> Cost of increasing capacity

3. Management of debtors

With the exception of some types of retailing, commercial sales are usually made on credit. As we have seen, this gives rise to time-lags in the transaction cycle of a business in so far as cash settlement lags some time behind the delivery of the goods or the rendering of the service to which the payment relates.

The main reasons for this practice are attributable to commercial convenience and, to some extent, to commercial tradition. It is seldom convenient for cash to be collected at the same time that goods are delivered for the following reasons:

- the recipient will need to assure himself that the goods are satisfactory prior to payment;
- additional security safeguards would need to be introduced with regard to the cash collected.

Even where it would be reasonably practicable to pay on

delivery, customers are reluctant to forego the traditional credit period since to do so would increase their own financing costs. The practice of allowing credit has thus come to be widely accepted as normal, though in many industries it need not be so.

The credit extended to a customer on sale is as much part of the deal as is the sale price or delivery date. The credit terms offered as standard to customers should be specifically considered as part of each business's periodic review of prices. For large deals, credit terms should be specifically negotiated.

The granting of credit has substantial costs associated with it. The management of debtors requires a clear determination of the business's policy and approach to the extension of credit based on a balanced view of competitor practice, the costs involved, and the risk of lost business:

- *Competitor practice:* This is the base line from which the business must start. In the absence of other factors, customers will expect normal industry terms to apply.
- *Costs of allowing credit:* These are the direct costs of granting customers time to pay. They include visible expenses such as interest and insurance cover, as well as invisible costs such as the risk of bad debts.
- *Costs of refusing credit:* These costs are more difficult to quantify, and include income foregone as a result of the refusal to extend credit.

Competitor practice

General practice determines customer expectations. Consequently, there is little room for departure from that practice without customer disenchantment, unless a business can offer other significant unique benefits to its customers. For example, a retail shop may offer lower prices than its competitors but may not accept payment by credit card (thus saving itself the card commissions and the admittedly short credit period taken by the credit card companies). Conversely, a business may offer extended credit in order to entice prospective customers. The car trade is an excellent example.

Costs of allowing credit

Certain costs will increase as the amount of credit (and thus the level of debtors) increases. Such costs include the following:

- Financing costs. These comprise the average amount due from customers multiplied by the organization's cost of capital.

- Costs of maintaining the necessary accounting records. It is necessary to keep a record of each customer showing how much is owed and for how long it has been owed.

- Costs of collecting the debts. Frequently debtors need to be reminded that cash is due to be paid. Even if only one letter or telephone call is needed to effect payment, that communication costs money. Debtors who, for one reason or another, show great reluctance to pay may have to be subjected to legal action to effect recovery of the debt.

- Bad debts. If a debtor cannot be made to pay, then the supplier not only loses his profit on the sale but has to bear the costs of the goods or service provided. However, the risk of bad debts may be covered by insurance, at a cost. Alternatively, goods may be sold under retention of title terms, whereby the vendor retains title to the goods until he is paid. In theory, in the event of default by the purchaser the vendor may recover those goods. In practice, recovery is more difficult.

- Cost of obtaining a credit reference. It is prudent when first granting credit to a new customer to take up references, usually from an agency which specializes in credit references.

- Discounts. As an inducement for debtors to pay promptly, businesses often offer their customers the right to deduct a small percentage (eg 2.5%) if they pay within a specified time from the date of sale.

- Inflation cost. Debtors which are outstanding during a period of inflation will lose value in terms of purchasing power since the amount subsequently paid will be worth less than it was when the debt was incurred.

Costs of refusing credit

These costs are more difficult to quantify, but include the following:

- Loss of customer goodwill. Since most businesses allow their customers credit, in the absence of compensating factors, a firm which refuses to allow credit will almost certainly find itself at a considerable disadvantage. The result will probably be a loss of trade.

- Inconvenience. Insisting on payment at the time of the supply of the goods or services may well lead to an increase in security risk, since cash will be collected by a large number of individual employees, rather than being received centrally.

The optimal level of debtors

As with the management of stocks, the two types of costs will need to be balanced in order to achieve a position of minimum total cost. In turn, that position has to be compared with normal trade practice in the industry in which the business operates. This is not an easy task and there are no simple mathematical models to offer guidance in this matter. However, assuming that a business does not go to the extreme of refusing to allow credit, there are several general rules which can be followed:

- Management should decide on its general policy towards allowing credit, based on a survey of industry norms. This policy-making stage should include consideration of such matters as the standard credit period allowed, whether an early settlement discount is to be offered, the possibility of selling under retention of title and the procedures to be adopted to follow up overdue debtors.

- All new customers should be assessed for creditworthiness and a permissible level of credit should be allocated to each. Their financial strength should be assessed based on published financial information or credit agency reports. If possible, trade references should be obtained to support the new customer's credibility and to prove that the required volumes of trade and proposed credit levels are not abnormal.

- The established credit levels should be rigidly adhered to unless a fundamental reappraisal of each customer's credit rating is undertaken.
- The ageing of debtors' accounts should be regularly reported and overdue debtors should be reminded that payment is due and pressed for payment, forcefully if necessary.

Management of creditors

Trade credit is a very important source of finance and in the case of many companies constitutes a substantial proportion of all the capital used. It is the cheapest form of finance since it has no cost attached to it. However, many companies allow cash discounts for early settlement of accounts payable, and the question arises whether it is better to take the discount and pay early, or to take the credit. Factors which influence this decision are:

- The terms on offer. The rule is that costs can be saved if the amount of discount on offer is greater than the cost of capital incurred by making the early payment. For example, a typical early settlement may be 2% for payment within 10 days. The alternative might be to take 45 days credit. In the case of a £10,000 account, taking the discount of 2% is worth £200. The cost of capital incurred to make this payment is the net 35 days credit foregone, which needs to be replaced by funds which carry a cost of capital. If the funds are borrowed from the bank at say 13%, the costs incurred are about £125. Thus it is worth taking the discount and paying early.
- The level of borrowings negotiated with bankers and general cash-flow position. The business may be running at or close to the limits of its borrowing capacity. As a result it may be unable to borrow money from the bank to take advantage of early settlement discounts.

There are other assets and liabilities which are included

in working capital, most of which are usually insignificant except for cash (or overdraft). Cash is generally of greatest importance when there is a shortage, and financing proposals and the financial design of a business are discussed in Chapter 8. Sources of funds have already been covered in Chapter 3.

Chapter 6

Managing business assets: capital projects

The capital assets of a business are fundamentally different from the working capital assets of that business.

Firstly, as we have seen in the previous chapter, investment in working capital assets is unavoidably incurred as a net result of the time-lags which exist in the transaction cycles of all businesses. Working capital investment liquidates itself and regenerates itself as a continuous process within the business. Each individual working capital asset has a relatively short life-span and is purchased in order to generate short-term profits. Secondly, there are generally a great many working capital assets, and their individual cost is low in relation to the total net worth of the business. Finally, and most importantly, usually the degree of commitment (and therefore, of risk) inherent within working capital assets is low since they are rapidly converted into cash.

By contrast, capital assets are purchased in the expectation of a worthwhile long-range return, in order to create that capacity which the business needs to be able to carry on its trade. That capacity will almost always be exploited over an extended business life which will certainly be much greater than the life of the working capital assets which pass through it. As a consequence the degree of commitment inherent within those capital assets is substantial. Furthermore, the purchase amounts involved may be large in value in relation to the net worth of the business, and may in turn generate substantial cash outflows and inflows and have other peripheral effects on the business as a whole.

The management of working capital assets is based predominantly on short-term considerations, since the lead-time for implementing changes is relatively short and mistakes can be corrected contemporaneously. However, the management of capital projects involves the raising of substantial sums of money which are then locked up in long-lived assets in the expectation of worthwhile future earnings. There is limited room for correcting mistakes which may appear once the project has been commenced.

As a result of all these factors the evaluation of capital projects has to take account of:

- the quality and reliability of information available about project costs and revenues, and the way in which uncertainties in that information might affect project success or failure;

- the time value of money. That is to say, the fact that in today's terms cash inflows in one or more year's time are worth less than their face value;

- whether projects are worthwhile. In other words, whether the financial performance of the project under consideration yields returns which are a net benefit to the business after financing costs and risk are considered;

- the priorities which should be allocated to projects, given that proposals may be mutually exclusive for a variety of reasons, including shortages of funds;

- the sources of funds which may be available to finance the capital projects, the cost of those funds and the repayment schedules which may be necessary.

1. Capital budgeting

Capital budgeting tackles the problem of the optimal allocation of investment funds within the business by considering the range of capital projects available to an enterprise, the total amount of capital expenditure which the enterprise can afford and the way in which the funding needs of these capital projects should be secured.

Typical capital budgeting decisions include:

- replacement and modernisation: for example, in a manufacturing environment, whether it is beneficial to replace existing facilities by more productive but more expensive plant; in a service environment, whether improvements in productivity by expenditure on efficiency aids such as computerisation of design or installation of comprehensive word processing facilities are likely to produce an acceptable return;

- expansion: whether it is beneficial to build and equip a new hotel or factory or to expand existing facilities;

- choice between alternative courses of action: in many instances, alternative courses of action are available to achieve a desired business result. However, the pattern of fund flows may differ substantially between those alternatives, and the financial returns earned may be significantly different;

- considering whether to buy outright or lease: leasing offers the opportunity for a business to defer till a later date payment of sizeable portions of the purchase price of an income-producing asset. It thus enables management to match incoming cashflows earned by the project with repayments of the capital involved. However, the buy outright alternative may permit the negotiation of discounts, payment deferrals or other benefits;

- financing problems: considering the effect of length of borrowing, repayment schedule and rate on the returns offered by the project, and on the borrowing capacity of the business as a whole.

2. The appraisal process

The approach adopted to capital appraisal relies on predicting the business consequences of accepting the investment proposal. Those consequences then have to be restated in terms of a unit of performance applicable to all projects, and compared with the minimum levels of performance acceptable to the business, and with the performance returns offered by other projects.

In order that a valid appraisal can be made, the future performance of the project under review has to be completely isolated from the performance of the rest of the business. That performance must then be appraised in a consistent and objective fashion. For those reasons most appraisal techniques focus on cash flows as a measure of project performance. Cash flows have the advantage that the incidence and amount of receipts or payments is clearly identifiable and can be measured objectively, whereas accounting profit is a relatively subjective composition of assumptions and conventions (as we have seen earlier). Furthermore, it is only cash that can be re-invested or paid out as dividends to the providers of capital.

The largest cash flow in nearly every project will be the initial outlay incurred to acquire the capital asset or to commence the project. Typically, this expenditure will be on tangible infrastructure assets such as land, buildings and machinery. It should be noted that depreciation and amortisation of such items are not cash outflows and thus are not relevant to assessment of future cash flows. However, other recurring cash outflows will arise on working capital items such as the purchase of stocks and the funding of debtors, less any credit which may be obtainable from suppliers. Cash disbursements for interest payments on capital borrowed for the project and repayments of principal are excluded in any evaluation of project cash flows. They are considered separately and differently in the different evaluation techniques.

Cash inflows arise in the main from project revenues. Revenues may be actual contributions, or alternatively may be the estimated value of incremental cost savings. Other cash inflows may arise from grants, from liquidation of working capital and from sales of project infrastructure assets at the end of the project life. On rare occasions projects may in their own right turn into self-contained businesses and might be sold or floated on the Stock Exchange, thus generating a substantial one-off cash inflow.

Taxation can be a significant cash outflow. Tax payments can be deferred by the incidence of certain tax allowances and the cash outlay itself takes place perhaps a year after the corresponding revenues are generated. These factors need to be considered properly in the cash flow.

The impact of future inflation over the long lifespan of a typical capital project can be very significant. Historically, high levels of inflation have correlated with high interest rates and (not unreasonably) with providers of capital demanding a high rate of monetary return from their investments. All of these factors introduce uncertainty into the forecasts. The way in which uncertainty can be approached is described in section 3 of this Chapter.

A number of different criteria can be generated to define the performance of proposed capital projects:

- accounting rate of return is the rate of book profit arising specifically on the net assets invested in the project;
- payback period is the time a project will take to generate sufficient cash to pay for itself;
- net present value assesses the value now of the sum of all future cash inflows and outflows attributable to the project;
- the internal rate of return is the true rate of return earned by the project.

Accounting rate of return

The accounting rate of return definition of project performance aims to describe in a single statistic the profit returned by a capital investment. The definition follows the lines of the interest available on an investment account at the bank or at a building society. In its common form, this measure is defined as:

average annual profit earned by the project
average capital employed within that project

In this context, profit is defined in its accounting sense as the income after charging all costs, including the depreciation of any capital expenditures involved. The average profit is simply defined as the total profit earned by the investment over the whole of its lifetime divided by that lifetime. Average capital can be more difficult to compute, since it is the sum over the project lifetime of the annual capital committed in the project, again divided by the total lifetime of the project. In practice, average capital is often half the original capital investment plus some working capital figure, since for many projects there is only one significant capital outlay incurred at the beginning which is fully written-off by the end.

Under this appraisal method, capital projects are acceptable only if their accounting rate of return is greater than some minimum level determined as part of the corporate strategic planning process. In the case of mutually exclusive projects, those with greater accounting rates of return are accepted before those with lower rates.

By way of example, consider a business faced with two alternative investment proposals, A & B. Both projects involve the purchase of machinery for £1,000,000 which for various valid reasons in both cases is likely to have an estimated useful life of above five years and a residual value of zero. In both cases the aggregate profit (after depreciation) over the project lifetime is expected to be £760,000.

However, the performance pattern of each project is different, as follows (£000s):

	PROJECT A		PROJECT B	
	Profit	Cashflow	Profit	Cashflow
Year 0	—	−1,000	—	−1,000
Year 1	10	190	230	600
Year 2	160	310	200	580
Year 3	160	410	160	530
Year 4	200	400	160	50
Year 5	230	450	10	—
	760	760	760	760

The average profits of each project are the same, at £152,000, and since the average sums invested are also the same at £500,000, the accounting rate of return of each project is also the same at 30.4%. Strictly, on the basis of the accounting rate of return criterion, both projects are equally acceptable.

However, in reality it is apparent that the projects are quite different. Although overall profitability is the same, the project cash flows are completely different since they have a completely different working capital requirement. Commonsense indicates that in fact the financial performance of each project differs substantially from that of the other because profits translate into useable, remittable earnings at completely different times. The simple accounting rate of return unit of performance fails to measure or convey that basic but important difference.

The accounting rate of return measure of project performance has certain advantages. It uses readily available accounting data, it is quick and easy to calculate, and the underlying concept is easy to grasp. However, its most serious drawbacks are that it does not take account of the timing of project yields, and that it uses subjective profit and balance-sheet investment data (rather than objective cash flows) to calculate the performance indicator. In addition, the accounting rate of return statistic fails to convey either the size or duration of a project. Thus, *prima facie*, a 30% return on £50,000 for two years might be preferred to a 15% return on £200,000 for five years.

For these reasons accounting rate of return is little used to measure and compare projects, or to trigger investment decisions. However, it is often used as a historical performance measuring device where its deficiencies can to some extent be overcome.

Payback period

This method of assessing project performance uses as a performance indicator the number of years over which the annual cash flows derived from the project will repay the capital investment.

To apply this method the cash flows arising from the project in each year of its life need to be calculated. By cash flows is meant the amount of cash which will be released from the project and which therefore will become available for investment elsewhere, or for return to the providers of capital. The payback point is reached when the cash inflows (including government grants, investment credits and the cash effect of tax allowances, if any) extinguish the initial cash input.

Under this appraisal method, capital projects are acceptable only if their payback period is less than some maximum period determined as part of the corporate strategic planning process. In the case of mutually exclusive projects, those with quicker payback are preferred.

Let us consider again the two projects set out in the previous section, which were of equal performance ranking according to the accounting rate of return criterion (£000s):

	PROJECT A		PROJECT B	
	Profit	*Cashflow*	*Profit*	*Cashflow*
Year 0	—	−1,000	—	−1,000
Year 1	10	190	230	600
Year 2	160	310	200	580
Year 3	160	410	160	530
Year 4	200	400	160	50
Year 5	230	450	10	—
	760	760	760	760

Project A will produce cash inflows aggregating £910,000 in the first 3 years, and so will pay for itself in about 3.25 years. On the same basis, project B will pay for itself in approximately 1.7 years. Since we know that both projects are equally profitable, it is sensible to prefer B as that project returns the initial investment more quickly and therefore exposes that investment to loss for less time.

Like the accounting rate of return, the payback method of measuring project performance has its advantages. It uses readily available accounting data, it is quick and easy to calculate, and the underlying concept is easy to grasp. It also takes into account, albeit in an unrigorous way, the fact that forecasts about the future become more and more unreliable the further forward they look.

One further important advantage is that this criterion introduces a maximum time horizon for project payback. On a strategic planning level, that time horizon can link in directly to business constraints such as expected product life, the availability of funds, the reaction time of competitors or the stability of a trading partner. For example, a business would probably not wish to proceed with a capital project to develop a new product which for competitive reasons could only be exploited in the market-place for three years if the payback period was two and a half years. In this case the margin for error and slippage might be considered too small.

The criterion has some serious disadvantages if it is used as a sole measure of project performance. Perhaps its most serious drawback is that it ignores cash flows which take place after the payback point has been reached, and it can therefore disadvantage projects which take time to reach maturity.

Consider projects A and C (£000s):

	PROJECT A		PROJECT C	
	Profit	Cashflow	Profit	Cashflow
Year 0	—	−1,000	—	−1,000
Year 1	10	190	130	600
Year 2	160	310	50	580
Year 3	160	410	0	0
Year 4	200	400	0	0
Year 5	230	450	0	0
	760	760	180	180

As we saw previously, project A will pay for itself in 3.25 years and project C in 1.7 years. But project A continues well beyond its payback point, whereas project C ceases almost immediately after payback.

Thus, rapid payback in itself cannot guarantee a superior profitability performance. In fact, this appraisal technique does not attempt to relate the total cash inflows of the project to the total cash outflows. Thus, it cannot serve as an indicator of overall project profitability.

Another important drawback is that in its simplest form the payback appraisal technique does not take account of the timing of project cash flows. Thus it is possible to have

equal payback performance ratings for two projects which
have a dissimilar pattern of cash flows.

Consider projects A and D (£000s):

| | PROJECT A | | PROJECT D | |
	Profit	*Cashflow*	*Profit*	*Cashflow*
Year 0	—	−1,000	—	−1,000
Year 1	10	190	130	800
Year 2	160	310	190	10
Year 3	160	410	220	100
Year 4	200	400	120	400
Year 5	230	450	100	450
	760	760	760	760

As we saw previously, project A will pay for itself in
3.25 years. Project D will pay for itself in the same time.
But the projects are not the same since the incidence of
cash inflows is completely different. That difference in
cash flows will have substantial implications for
borrowing levels and the cost of borrowing.

The costs of funding can be reflected in the project
performance measure by charging a notional interest on
the net uncleared project balance and adding that to the
balance which must be paid back by the project.

Consider projects A and D again (£000s):

Interest rate of 10%   PROJECT A

	Cashflow	*Net balance*	*Notional interest*	*New balance*
Year 0	−1,000	−1,000	−100	−1,100
Year 1	190	−910	−91	−1,001
Year 2	310	−691	−69	−760
Year 3	410	−350	−35	−385
Year 4	400	15	n/a	n/a
Year 5	450	n/a	n/a	n/a
	760			

PROJECT D

	Cashflow	*Net balance*	*Notional interest*	*New balance*
Year 0	−1,000	−1,000	−100	−1,100
Year 1	800	−300	−30	−330
Year 2	10	−320	−32	−352
Year 3	100	−252	−25	−277
Year 4	400	123	n/a	n/a
Year 5	450	n/a	n/a	n/a
	760			

117

On this more realistic basis, the payback period of project A is just under four years, whereas the payback period of project D is three years and eight months.

A final difficulty is that if payback is used alone, one might lose sight of the absolute size of the investment. Thus a payback period of 2 years on a £10,000 investment may be preferred to a payback period of 3 years on a £500,000 investment.

The payback performance criterion is capable of providing some measured insight into project risk and into the level of commitment inherent in projects. Therefore, based on a business's strategic posture it is possible to specify minimum payback periods within which all acceptable projects have to fall. However, the criterion in itself is not sufficiently broad to allow it to form the sole basis for detailed selection of a capital project portfolio. For those reasons, the payback performance criterion is used only as a complementary capital project appraisal yardstick.

Discounted cash flow

The previous two methods of appraising project performance had a number of significant shortcomings because they neglected to deal with the timing and size of cash flows during a project's life. Discounted cash flow techniques of project performance appraisal take both these factors into account.

The fundamental ingredient of any financially successful project is that the return arising is greater than the investment located in that project. But returns typically relate to the future, whereas outlays need to be made now: and the value of money in a year's time or more is less than that of the same amount of money now. Thus the time value of money needs to be taken into account if a valid assessment is to be made of the relationship between investment and return.

The discounted cash flow appraisal technique takes account of the time value of money by substituting a present value for each of the project's future cash movements. The present value is nothing other than the value now of those future cash transactions. This process of substitution results in a series of cash flows, all of which are denominated in the same units of measure (present value currency). As a consequence, they can be validly added, subtracted, compared and otherwise used mathematically.

The net present value project performance criterion calculates the difference between the present value of cash inflows and outflows over the project life in order to determine the desirability of a project. If the net present value of a project is greater than zero then the discounted cash inflows are greater than the discounted cash outflows, and the project is beneficial. If the net present value is less than zero, then the discounted cash outflows are greater than the discounted cash inflows and the project is not worthwhile. If the net present value is equal to zero, then the flows balance each other out and there is neither loss nor gain.

Present value: The present value of a cash transaction has already been defined as the value now of that future transaction. The value now of a future transaction is arrived at by discounting future cash flows for the effect of the earning capability of money over the relevant period of time:

> If an organisation has £1,000 to invest and places that money in a fixed term interest-bearing account carrying interest at 10% per annum, compounded annually, then the capital value of that sum will increase as follows:

> | | |
> |---|---|
> | Initial investment | 1,000 |
> | At end of first year | 1,100 |
> | At end of second year | 1,210 |
> | At end of third year | 1,331 |
> | Etc. . . . | |

Thus to this organisation, the value now at a rate of interest of 10% of £1,100 to be received in a year's time is £1,000. Similarly, the value now at that rate of interest of £1,210 to be received in two years' time is also £1,000. In general, the value now of any sum receivable at a future date (given a set interest rate) is termed the present value of that sum. The rate of interest is more commonly referred to as the discount rate for reasons which will be discussed later.

It can be seen from the example that in order to define present value a discount rate has to be defined for the project as a whole and that each future cash transaction has to have a defined transaction date and an identifiable amount.

In practice, discount factors are calculated and set out in tables or embodied within standard calculation routines in calculators so as to be easily applied to projected cash flows. Thus, for each discount rate, the discount factors are expressed by year as the factor which should be applied to future cash flows in order to discount them to present value. For example, for the cash flows already seen above:

10% Discount rate

	Capital amount	Discount factor	Present value
Initial investment	1,000	1	1,000
At end of first year	1,100	.909	1,000
At end of second year	1,210	.826	1,000
At end of third year	1,331	.751	1,000

(these may be all verified by calculator—for example 1,000 divided by 1,210 equals .826)

Discount factors can be very high if rates are high or if a project has an extended life.

For example, many insurance companies promise what seem to be huge sums of money at a specified time in the future in return for regular monthly premiums. Would it be a good deal if such an offer promised say £60,000 in 25 years time in return for a single premium payment now of £10,000?

The present value of £60,000 in 25 years time at various discount rates—

Discount rate	Discount factor	Present value
3%	.48	28,600
5%	.3	18,000
7%	.18	10,800
8%	.15	9,000
10%	.09	5,400
15%	.03	1,800
20%	.01	600

Whether the investment is a good deal or not depends on the view you would have on the discount rate. In this case, the discount rate could be the interest rate that the money could earn or cost elsewhere or perhaps the rate of inflation.

The investment would certainly not be worth making unless inflation was less than 7%. Inflation at a rate greater than 7% erodes away the value of the future £60,000 so that its present value is less than the amount invested. The money would be better spent on tangible assets which would have a better chance of keeping their value.

If one were to borrow the money specifically for this transaction the discount rate would be the rate payable on the borrowing. If that were less than 7% a net return on the transaction would be achieved.

If the money could be invested elsewhere that would be preferable if a return of better than 7% could be obtained.

It should be emphasised that the primary objective of this process of discounting is to reflect the normal commercial ability of money to earn more money (interest) and the requirement for any investment to earn a minimum acceptable rate of return (often called the hurdle rate). It does not necessarily have anything to do with inflation, although inflation may be a factor which has to be built into the discount factor to be used (see later).

Net present value: The net present value of a capital project is the value of the sum of all future cash inflows and cash outflows discounted back at an appropriate rate to a common date.

The essential ingredients for a net present value appraisal are:

- a suitable discount rate appropriate to the project;
- forecast annualised project cash flows.

Once the data is available, the appraisal technique is easily applied.

Consider again projects A, B and D, with a discount rate based on specific borrowing for the project at 12%:

PROJECT A

	Cashflow	Discount factor	Present value
Year 0	−1,000	1	−1,000
Year 1	190	.89	169
Year 2	310	.8	248
Year 3	410	.71	291
Year 4	400	.64	256
Year 5	450	.57	256
	760	Net present value	220

PROJECT B

	Cashflow	Discount factor	Present value
Year 0	−1,000	1	−1,000
Year 1	600	.89	534
Year 2	580	.8	464
Year 3	530	.71	376
Year 4	50	.64	32
Year 5	—	.57	—
	760	Net present value	406

PROJECT D

	Cashflow	Discount factor	Present value
Year 0	−1,000	1	−1,000
Year 1	800	.89	712
Year 2	10	.8	8
Year 3	100	.71	71
Year 4	400	.64	256
Year 5	450	.57	256
	760		303

The net present value of project B exceeds that of project A and that of D, and thus if the projects were mutually exclusive, B would be preferred.

Under conditions where the availability of funds is not

limited, and where risk is uninsured, the decision rule based on this criterion is to accept all projects which have a positive net present value using the cost of the extra funds required for the project as the discount factor. In practice, projects may compete for funds, and other considerations such as the time profile of cash flows and degree of risk will influence selection. In particular, risk will increase the returns required of a project. The impact of risk is discussed later on in this Chapter.

Where funds are limited, selection of projects becomes much more complex. In the simplest instance, where a limited capital budget is available to fund a number of projects, a simple profitability index can be generated to compare the various returns available. Such a profitability index connects the net present value of project cash inflows with the initial cash investment, thus:

$$\frac{\text{net present value of cash inflows}}{\text{initial cash investment}}$$

The greater the value of this profitability index above one, the greater the desirability of the project.

Where capital constraints are likely to arise during project lifetimes rather than at commencement it is necessary generally to use computer modelling to determine which projects can be accommodated. This can be done as part and parcel of the measurement of the reactions of the project to changes in external economic conditions. (See later in this Chapter for a discussion of the impact of risk and uncertainty).

The main advantages of the net present value method of project appraisal is that it provides a rigorous analytical framework which links an assessment of future project performance with the costs of funding that project, while at the same time allowing latitude for more sophisticated analysis. The main disadvantage is that it is often not understood by businessmen.

Internal rate of return

The internal rate of return of a project is defined as the

discount factor which makes that project's net present value equal to nil. In other words, the internal rate of return is the notional cost of funds at which the project generates breakeven returns.

To appraise whether specific projects are worth undertaking, the internal rate of return of those projects has to be compared with the cost of providing the funding for those projects. Clearly, the projects are worthwhile if the internal rate of return is higher than the cost of funds. They are not worth proceeding with if the internal rate of return is lower.

Consider again projects A, B and D:

	PROJECT A Cashflow	PROJECT B Cashflow	PROJECT D Cashflow
Year 0	−1,000	−1,000	−1,000
Year 1	190	600	800
Year 2	310	580	10
Year 3	410	530	100
Year 4	400	50	400
Year 5	450	—	450
	760	760	760
Net present value at —			
12%	220	406	303
17%	64	294	172
19%	10	253	126
20%	−15	234	105
25%	−128	143	9
26%	−149	126	−8
34%	−287	7	−127
35%	−302	−7	−140
Internal rate of return (approximately)	19%	34%	25%

This method of measuring project performance shares all the advantages offered by the net present value method. It also yields in familiar form a performance statistic which is directly comparable against the cost of project funds and which provides an indication of surplus of yield over that cost.

The main difficulty with the internal rate of return criterion is that it assumes that the cash flows generated by the project (at whatever the internal rate of return may be) are immediately reinvested in further projects which yield that same internal rate of return. Although that assumption rarely holds true, most internal rates of return are close enough to the cost of capital to enable cash generated to be regarded substantially as discharging capital liabilities in the same way as cash flows generated under the net present value criterion.

3. The impact of risk and uncertainty

Since project appraisal involves the assessment and evaluation of the future, that process unavoidably encounters uncertainty. To cope with that uncertainty, financial engineers must:

- understand the causes of risk;
- appreciate their organisation's attitude to risk;
- be able to quantify the effect of uncertainty on the projects that they are proposing (ie the degree of risk);
- recommend action.

The causes of risk

In financial analysis risk arises as a consequence of imperfect information: for example, the revenues anticipated from a project are estimates and only time will show whether they have been accurately assessed or not. The evaluation of risk considers the likelihood of deviation from the expected result, and the consequences on project viability of such deviation.

Risk can be split into two principal areas:

- *project risk*, which might be better described as the relative uncertainty relating to the success or failure of alternative ventures in a particular industrial sector. For example, it may be feasible to drill for oil in a number of specific locations. The cost of investigating each location is different, as is the likelihood of finding useable reserves of oil. Thus the risk/reward relationship varies from project to project. This type of risk is linked to succeed/fail conditions;

- *market risk*, which could be defined as the inherent instability of any given business sector. For example, the oil prospecting ventures described above might be successful in finding oil, but a change in market conditions might make the exploitation of that find uneconomic. These types of risk arise from "market fickleness".

The distinction between the two types of risk is important, since they are approached in different ways:

- Project risk is approached on a portfolio basis, whereby it is expected that there will be a limited number of successful projects produced out of all of those on hand. Clearly the profitability and cash flow of the successful survivors has to be high, since they must both compensate for the losses incurred on the failures and provide the overall returns which are required.
- Market risk is approached by accepting only those projects which provide sufficient cushion in the expected returns to accommodate downturns in trade or possible cycling of markets due to fashion changes etc.

Attitude to risk

Effective decision making requires an understanding of risk preferences. Decision makers rarely feel that they have a complete knowledge of the likely outcome of a business decision. For that reason an understanding of the house style and the inclination (or disinclination) of the organisation to risk are important. Different organisations have different attitudes to risk:

- *aversion:* such organisations choose safe projects. Their project selection criterion is to select from the range available only those projects which under a worst case condition exceed a certain minimum level of profitability (see below);
- *seeking:* such organisations choose projects which offer superlative returns and pay little regard to the risks of failure;

● *norm:* the essence of this attitude to risk is that the organisation wishes to select that project which, in the event that it proves not the right project to have chosen, produces the lowest cost differential (or lowest income foregone) from that which the optimal choice would have produced (see below).

Consider these organisations faced with the choice of selecting one of three mutually exclusive projects. Assessment of the projects has been made under a variety of economic conditions, and the likely outcomes in terms of net present value are given below (£000s) —

PROJECT	*Possible economic scenario*			
	1	2	3	4
Project A	500	300	140	0
Project B	340	280	200	100
Project C	160	160	160	160

Style of organisation	*Selection criterion*	*Project selected*
Aversion	maximize minimum level of contribution (ie in the worst possible case we will have a net present value of 160)	C
Seeking	maximize maximum level of contribution (ie if everything goes right we will have a net present value of 500)	A
Norm	minimize net present value loss — see below for explanation*	A or B

*If A is selected and B should have been selected then the maximum opportunity loss is 100. If A is selected and C should have been selected then the maximum loss is 160.

If B is selected and C should have been selected then the maximum opportunity loss is 60. If B is selected and A should have been selected then the maximum loss is 160.

If C is selected and B should have been selected then the maximum opportunity loss is 180. If C is selected and A should have been selected then the maximum loss is 340.

Selection of either project A or B gives a maximum income loss of 160, which is the lowest maximum income loss available.

This form of matrix analysis is useful for presentation purposes, when it can be used to demonstrate the consequences of different development strategies. For example, a retail store chain may consider three options:

- expansion into a specific and perhaps unstable market segment. For example, high fashion boutiques, which will do well unless there is an economic downturn. If there is an economic downturn, then they will do very badly indeed.

- expansion into products related to the lines which are currently carried, but which are fashion-related and new to the chain. The margins on these products are commensurate with those on the product ranges currently carried, but the introduction of the new lines into stores will also pull new customers into those stores. Because of the spread of customers, the extremes of high profit or high loss under the different possible economic scenarios are avoided.

- expansion of store selling areas, but no change in product lines carried. This strategic move should lead to a low but reliable increase in profit and little, if any, swing in performance in the event of changed economic conditions.

These three options equate to Projects A, B and C respectively, above. Quantification of the results of each project under varying economic scenarios and presentation in the matrix form already outlined can be a useful portrayal of the risk reward relationship of the projects.

Quantification of the effect of uncertainty

In business, often the outcome of a selected course of action cannot be predicted with certainty since it depends on factors which vary at random. Under those conditions, probability theory provides a means of evaluating the likelihood of given outcomes.

Probabilities can be:

- objective — based on past performance history. For example, semiconductor chip failures in the electronics industry, sales performance or bad debts in mail order retailing.

● subjective — based on management's considered knowledge of the business. For instance, an assessment that a new private hospital has a 60% chance of achieving a certain level of occupancy within a given period of time.

In either case the whole of the potential outcome can be expressed as a distribution of probabilities. For instance, the possible cash flows in year 1 from an investment project of £10,000 might range from £1,000 (unlikely) through £3,000 (most likely) to £5,000 (unlikely). Those possible outcomes can be shown graphically as follows:

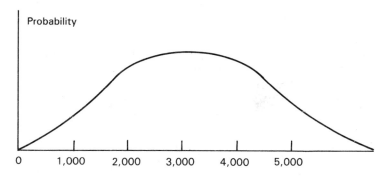

The same graph might be applied to the net present values of a series of projects, in order to show what might be the spread of possible outcomes, and what the relative probabilities of achieving those outcome might be. It may be that two projects have the same maximum net present value, but that the probabilities (or chance) of achieving that value are different.

Consider again the investment project above (Project A) and contrast it with another investment project, also of £10,000 (Project B), which has the same maximum net present value.

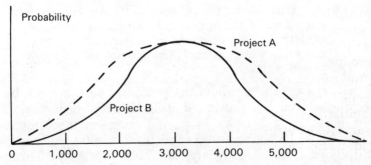

Project B has a smaller spread of outcomes with a significant probability of occurrence, and therefore there is a greater chance of an outcome close to the maximum. Project A has the same maximum outcome, but the spread is greater, and hence the chance of an outcome close to the maximum is less.

The wider the spread of outcomes, the greater the risk of an unpredicted outcome. Thus the spread, or dispersion, of any range of possible outcomes is a measure of the uncertainty inherent within the project.

The conventional statistic used to measure dispersion is known as standard deviation. Standard deviation is defined as:

$$\sigma = \sqrt{\text{(probability of each outcome} \times \text{(the value of that outcome} - \text{the value of the expected outcome)}}$$

The σ of a net present value distribution is a measure of the perceived uncertainty inherent within the project.

In practice, difficulties arise in determining the dispersion of net present values. The business events involved may be highly complex and may interact and be mutually dependent. Very often the causal relationships between events are understood, but the actual patterns in which they occur are impossible to predict.

In such cases, the business can be modelled or simulated by constructing an analogue of the situation with all the financial relationships defined as they are understood. This kind of model can easily be constructed using one of the many "spreadsheet" modelling packages which are

130

available for nearly all microcomputers. Then, if the range of driving independent variables is known (which will usually be the case), the analogue can be used to produce a range of outputs which in turn can be used to produce the required financial data.

Sensitivity analysis is a technique complementary to simulation. Usually, it is necessary to freeze some of the variable components of a business or a project before it can be modelled. Clearly, the frozen variables should not be those which are crucial to the success or failure of the project. Sensitivity analysis measures the impact on net present values of the variation of each of the independent driving variables, and, if necessary, confirms that the correct variables have been frozen.

Recommending action

Decision making under conditions of uncertainty involves the determination of:

- the sets of alternatives available;
- a range of possible outcomes of each alternative;
- the probability of each outcome occurring;
- an assessment of the overall likely benefits of each alternative;
- an assessment of the possible costs if the project is not a success.

It is not usually difficult to define feasible sets of alternatives since they are usually determined by the business. Ranges of possible outcomes can be derived by theoretical calculation, or more commonly, by simulation techniques. Unless some form of performance history is available, it is much more difficult to assign probabilities to outcomes. Frequently, they have to be assigned subjective probabilities assessed by management.

Under these conditions, market risk can be catered for by increasing the required project performance by a factor which compensates for the dispersion of possible outcomes. In the case of discounted cash flow assessment, discount rates can be regarded as being made up of two components which must be varied as necessary:

- risk-free or normal-risk rate of return (ie normal market rate earned by the business)

  plus

- risk premium attaching to the particular project (sufficient to provide adequate returns to cushion uncertainties and reward risk-taking).

For project risk, a useful concept is to treat the result of the expected outcome of an alternative and its assigned probability as a notional value of that course of action. For example:

> Farr & Co Limited are a national chain of stationers, bookshops and newsagents. They are currently enjoying an exceptionally good year, and to build on success, are considering the development of a chain of all-night city-centre bookshops specially catering for insomniacs. Forecasts with sensitivity analysis of results have shown that for the first such bookshop the failure net present value will be −£1,000,000. The expected level of incremental net present value of the project is expected to be +£4,000,000. The board of Farr & Co has reviewed the project proposals, and is split. One faction consider the idea to be ludicrous, whereas the other think that it is worth trying in the light of the company's current good financial health. The board has reached a consensus view that the project has a less than even chance of success (subjectively judged to be a 40% chance of success and a 60% chance of failure).
>
> The expected value of this project can be shown as follows:

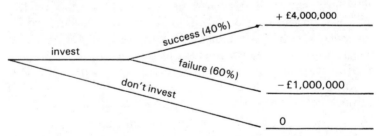

> The expected value of proceeding with the project is 40% x £4,000,000 − 60% x £1,000,000, which is equal to +£1,000,000. The expected value of not proceeding is 0. On this basis the project is worth trying.

The power of the expected value approach is that it can be further developed to include projects which are dependent on the success of the first project. If the Farr bookshop were to be a pilot for a whole chain, and if, given that the first one was successful, the rate of success thereafter was 60% rather than the initial 40%, the expected value would be much enhanced:

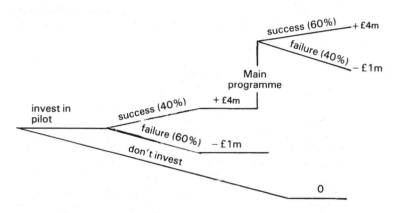

The range of expected values would be as follows:

Action	Outcome	Expected value
Don't invest in pilot	n/a	0
Invest in pilot	Failure	−600,000
	Success (pilot only)	1,600,000
Expected value, pilot only		1,000,000
Invest in main	Failure	−400,000
programme (per shop)	Success	2,400,000
Expected value, shop only		2,000,000
Total expected value of proceeding		
Pilot only		1,800,000
Shop only 2,000,000 × 40%		800,000
Total expected value		2,600,000

An alternative way of approaching the same problem is to flex the success/failure probabilities until the project breaks even, and then to see whether the subjective chances of success exceed the calculated figure.

This expected value approach can be applied to any

situation where there is uncertainty about the outcome of specific events. It is particularly useful for budgeting or forecasting.

For example, a sales budget may be broken down by potential customer (or market, or country or whatever is meaningful) (units):

Customer	Prior year order	Current year Indicated by customer	Current year Assessed likelihood	Budget
A	3,600	5,000	80%	4,000
B	2,221	2,000	50%	1,000
C	1,010	1,500	80%	1,200
D	559	300	10%	30
E	480	500	100%	500
F	430	500	100%	500
Other	800	800	120%	960
	9,100	10,600		8,190

This sales budget can easily be translated into contribution using the techniques discussed in Chapter 5. (Note that sales budgets can go down as well as up!). If the sales budget is for a new product or project it can be translated into cash flows and used in a discounted cash flow appraisal.

Finally, in any but the simplest capital project appraisals it is sensible to assess the bail-out cost. In its simplest form, this is simply the cost of abandoning the project in the event of failure.

Chapter 7

Control and analysis of performance

Just as assets and liabilities are divided into short term working capital and long term infrastructure, so too, the control of business performance has to be sub-divided into techniques which deal respectively with the shorter and the longer term:

- the optimisation of long range performance is concerned with what resources are to be created, when, how and for what purpose;
- short term control of performance is geared to ensuring that the business's existing resources are used in the best possible way.

1. Optimising long range performance

The last Chapter stressed uncertainty and the lack of knowledge about the longer term future. Long range planning is an attempt to reduce that uncertainty by:

- setting well defined goals or corporate objectives for the business enterprise;
- and by defining the business strategies required to achieve those goals.

Corporate objectives

Setting corporate objectives is a simple and very difficult process.

It is a simple process because there are usually very few

goals, and they can be expressed simply and concisely. For example, the shareholders of a family business may decide that for whatever reason, they want to go to the Unlisted Securities Market in three years' time. The management of a public company will probably wish to maintain growth in dividends and earnings for shareholders.

It is a difficult process, because a consensus view is required from the top management and probably the shareholders. Furthermore, it is not easy to create and keep clear sight of a distant objective when all around are the everyday matters of a complex business.

Business strategies

Defining business strategies is a rather easier process. Strategies are ways in which the business can be conducted in order to fulfill the corporate objectives. For example, the family company referred to earlier may need to have an earnings growth and a management development strategy to meet its goal of entering the Unlisted Securities Market. The public company may need to change or develop product lines, enter new markets, make acquisitions or incur research and development expenditure whilst at the same time generating an increased amount of cash in order to maintain its dividend and earnings growth.

Corporate planning is the term used to describe the process through which first corporate goals and then the strategies required to achieve them are developed.

Corporate planning is above all a process of identifying the need for change, and initiating and managing that change in an orderly fashion over the longer term. Thus the first step in this long range planning process is to identify the need to change and the targets for which the business will aim.

The second step, that of initiating change, involves a definition of the strategies by means of which the corporate targets will be reached. In turn, that definition requires a thorough knowledge of those elements of the economic environment which affect the operations of the business, and an understanding of the way in which they combine to create opportunities or threats. At the same time, the skills and other attributes of the business and its deficiencies and weaknesses need to be assessed.

This comprehensive evaluation of the business "warts an' all" is often termed SWOT analysis (Strengths: Weaknesses: Opportunities: Threats). Based on this evaluation of the business and its environment, business strategies can be evolved to move it towards its corporate goals by capitalising on opportunities and strengths. Additional strategies may need to be developed to eliminate weaknesses and to counter threats.

The final step is to manage the change. That process involves devolving the strategies selected as part of step two into short range actions. Typically, that involves translating the rather global strategic planning statements into more detailed budgets which can be understood and implemented by line managers.

In summary, the whole process revolves around the SWOT analysis:

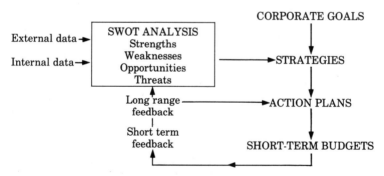

Consider how such a process might work at the family company, Krystell Limited. Krystell Limited is owned by the directors. It has grown rapidly from modest beginnings to a turnover of about £1,800,000 and has profits after tax of about £120,000.

That company, which is based in London, buys and sells high quality crystalware. The crystalware is manufactured entirely in the United Kingdom, but sales are made almost exclusively into export markets in Germany and the USA. In the main, the buyers are specialist dealers.

The shareholders of the company have for their individual reasons decided that their aim will be to realise some of the wealth that they have locked up in that business. In their view, the best way of achieving that aim is to get the company to the Unlisted Securities Market within the next 3 or 4 years. That is their global objective for the business.

Considerable effort will need to be expended in the next few years to make the company a suitable prospect for the USM. That effort will be channelled into the strategies which need to be employed to exploit the opportunities presented to the company and its strengths, while at the same time countering threats and eliminating weaknesses. In other words having decided upon their goal, the directors will have to perform a SWOT analysis.

What does the SWOT analysis show? In this particular case, the strengths of the company include loyal customers and a good trade reputation, the skill of generating the right product and the ability to respond quickly to the needs of the market-place. However, the company is heavily dependent on its single speciality product line, where adequacy of supplies can be a problem. In addition, it also depends on one substantial customer who provides a third of the total turnover and all of the net profit. Financial systems are weak and there is little if any financial management.

Opportunities which present themselves include a trend in the end-user market-place towards a more fashion-based approach to glassware of all kinds. This is particularly true of the young urban professionals. As a result, the customers of the company should experience greater demand for specialist crystal and glassware. In addition, at the highest quality end of the market, increasing scarcity of antique pieces may create a new market for new reproduction product.

Threats are predominantly linked to the export nature of the company's trade, and the vulnerability that creates to exchange rates, import control, political decrees etc.

Based on these assessments, and on other factors the directors will set out their strategies in terms of action plans.

The outline action plans might read as follows:

We aim to grow turnover to £3,600,000 and net profit to £500,000 over the next three years, while at the same time funding all of this growth from internally generated funds. We aim to do this by —

1. Expanding the market in the USA for our existing line.

2. Adding sympathetic factored product lines to that which we carry, and marketing them to our existing customers.

3. Investing in a manufacturing facility to hand-craft the high quality crystalware which we should be able to sell to our existing customers.

4. Adding service to our products by emphasising customer satisfaction, quality of packaging and accuracy of order-filling.

5. Establishing a business infrastructure capable of supporting the proposed level of activity. That includes not only investing in the physical infrastructure, but also recruiting financial management and installing computerised reporting systems.

Many other possible strategies leap to mind. They may not all be capable of implementation, and they may not all be successfully implemented: but their essence is that they are a statement of how the company might achieve its goal. They have to be purged of impractical ideas, or strategies which cannot be followed due to resource constraints, leaving behind a set of strategies which are suitable for implementation and which need to be turned into detailed short-term budgets.

2. Control of short term performance

Corporate and strategic planning is concerned with the long range goals of the business and the way in which it has to change its strategic position in order to reach them. Such change takes much time to implement fully, and the objectives and techniques which measure achievement are relatively global in nature. Short term performance needs to be planned and controlled in greater detail.

In any substantial business, effective control over short term performance can only be established if the structure of the organization is such that responsibility and authority over related elements of the business can be linked and delegated. If that organizational framework is in place, then the business strategies developed through the corporate planning process can be allocated to the relevant parts of the organization in terms of detailed operating objectives.

Thus, the essential components of any short term planning and control system include:

- a long range plan of which an integral part is a set of short range goals detailed enough to relate to specific areas of business activity;
- an organizational structure which permits the establishment of logical and accountable business activity centres (profit centres, cost centres, departments etc);
- an organizational ethos which permits the matching of responsibility and authority, so that the managers responsible for given business activity centres participate in the goal-setting process, and have the authority to react quickly and effectively to problems at their own discretion;
- a management reporting system which reflects the organizational structure of the business, which reports the right information in the right format to the right manager and which is understood by management.

If any of these ingredients is missed out there is a danger that the control system will prove ineffective. It will either be too cumbersome and inflexible to work, or it will be resented as an imposition by line management.

If the ingredients are present, then the installation and the operation of a short term planning and control system is very simple:

Setting short term goals such as detailed turnover,
profit and cost targets

↓

Agreeing allocation of responsibilities

↓

Monitoring performance against plan

↓

Explaining and reacting to deviations from plan

This four-step process is called budgetary control.

Setting short term goals

Short term goals have to be defined in actionable terms, by responsible units. Thus the master budget for a business may have as many subsidiary budgets as is appropriate.

For example, the components of the budget prepared by a manufacturing company will include:

- *the sales budget,* which assesses the customer take-up of the company's products and the cost of selling and distributing those products;
- *the production budget,* which uses the product volumes identified in the sales budget to plan what is to be made and when, to detect any potential capacity constraints, and to identify what purchases of raw materials are needed;
- *the personnel budget,* which uses the levels of physical activity predicted in the sales and production areas to plan the manpower needs of the company;
- *the administration budget,* which assesses the likely establishment costs needed to support the predicted level of business;
- *the master budget,* which will summarise the previous budgets and which will predict the operating profit or loss of the business, its cash generation or usage, financial costs, such as interest, and the balance-sheet position.

Limiting factors

Most businesses are limited by market demand. For that reason budgets usually start with sales as the independent variable. However, if the business is otherwise constrained, then the budgeting process should start off with an attempt to optimise the use of the limiting factor.

For example:

- a hotel which is generally full would try to improve

its earnings by turning away low rate contract guests (eg tours) in order to create room for premium rate business customers;

- a manufacturing company which is producing at full capacity should try to improve its earnings by placing marketing emphasis on those products which provide a greater contribution and by increasing prices on other products;

- a design consultancy which has no spare designer time to sell and which is unable to hire the right quality of additional design staff should improve its earnings by increasing prices, and by reviewing the activities of consultants to determine whether any of their time was spent on unnecessary and delegable work.

A limiting factor is any aspect of a company's business which cannot be increased above some amount. The most common examples of limiting factors are:

- cash and credit availability;
- plant capacity;
- labour availability;
- raw materials availability.

Zero based budgeting

Most budgets are prepared using historical performance as a guide to the future. This is a useful and practical approach, but it also has a hidden danger. That danger is that bad practice and inefficiency can be repeated and perpetuated. In order to expunge bad habits, zero-based budgets can be prepared which build up costs on a no-assumption basis from the underlying physical activities. This kind of exercise can be done once every few years and often yields surprisingly valuable results.

There is one final point to remember when preparing the master budget. In general, the fixed costs of a business remain constant as that business increases its level of activity. Consequently, those fixed costs decrease as a proportion of revenues, and the net profit per unit sold increases. However, when the business reaches a level where throughput starts to exceed the capacity of its infrastructure an increase in fixed costs may be necessary. If a business is operating in this region of its capacity, then increases in sales can well result in a drop in profitability and cash generation. This is illustrated below:

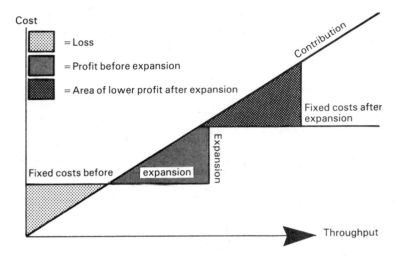

Agreeing allocation of responsibilities

As well as setting out a plan for the future, budgets should set out authority and responsibility for performance of activities.

Responsibility accounting is one method by which top management can delegate responsibility for budget achievement. It results in a lower level of management being responsible for controlling the business of their department in response to the approved budget. Responsibility accounting involves the specific allocation within simple guidelines of total authority over functional areas to managers.

The basic stages in establishing a responsibility accounting system are as follows:

● determine the budget functional centres;
● prepare budgets for each functional centre;

143

- discuss these budgets with appropriate department heads and amend if necessary;
- department heads then are responsible for explaining differences between actual and budgeted results for their own functional centre.

There are a number of essential points to consider and resolve if such a system is to be successfully employed:

- does the department manager actually have control over the resources and expenses allocated to his department?
- is the profit or cost centre well defined?
- is the profit or cost centre self-contained? (or do its activities affect the activities of another/is it affected by another's activities?)

The allocation of responsibilities will vary depending on the type of business and its style of operation. A typical split of responsibilities might be:

— *Sales director*	Sales volume
	Selling prices
	Selling expenses
	Marketing expenses
	Levels of finished stock on hand
— *Works director*	Raw material purchases
	Raw material stocks
	Labour costs
	Factory overheads
	Levels of work-in-progress
— *Finance director*	Office salaries
	Office overheads
	Capital expenditure budget
	Cash forecasting

In practice many activities overlap departments. Responsibility for budget control must therefore be clearly defined.

Monitoring performance against plan

Control is only meaningful if a credible relevant yardstick exists with which measurement can be made. In the case of budgetary control, actual performance is being measured against the plan. If variations are small, like is being measured against like, and useful information can be obtained from those variations. However, if variations are enormous (for instance, throughput was planned to be 160,000 units but actual is running at 80,000), the entire basis of the plan is undermined, and comparison becomes meaningless (other than as a message that something is seriously awry).

Thus the plan should be kept up to date and revised periodically to take account of the effect of significant unplanned operating changes. At the financial level, this can be done quite easily if the plan is prepared in the first instance on a basis which distinguishes between variable and fixed costs. Clearly, fixed costs will remain essentially constant, regardless of throughput changes, whereas variable costs will alter.

The differences between actual and plan need to be analysed to reveal the causes of the differences. Management reports should be designed so as to show principal cost/revenues constituents by type so that differences are capable of meaningful analysis and interpretation. Typical variances (by function) are —

Purchasing	
Materials —	price
Production	
Materials —	usage
Labour —	rate
	efficiency
	idle time
Overhead —	capacity utilisation
	spend
Sales —	price
	mix

Explaining and reacting to deviations from plan

Deviations can be identified by:

- horizontal variance analysis, which compares current period performance (balance sheet and profit and loss) with prior history and budget;

- vertical variance analysis, which compares profit and loss items with the relevant balance sheet items.

Both of these techniques can be usefully combined through analysis of operating ratios.

Ratios permit comparison of linked, causally-related business events. They can thus pinpoint problems and provide an excellent, overall measure of performance in predetermined key areas. Furthermore, useful "industry-norm" performance statistics can be obtained from published accounts (see also Chapter 9). These can be used to plan goal statistics for any business, and to determine whether problems which are being experienced are internal only or perhaps industry-wide.

Ratio analysis techniques are described in the next section.

3. Ratio analysis of management accounts

Any ratio expresses the relationship between two financial features of a business. Comparative performance is much better measured in terms of ratios because business performance can best be judged in terms of the relationships between causally related financial facts.

> For example, sales might increase by £2,000,000 per annum resulting in an increase in operating profit of £100,000 and an increase in average debtors of £1,000,000. Is this good or bad?

> In fact it is impossible to answer this question without further information. If the previous relationship between debtors and sales was significantly less than the relationship between the incremental amounts, then the quality of the extra business would be in doubt. If the extra profit earned covered the interest charges incurred on the capital borrowed to finance the new debtors, and the new sales were unlikely to generate bad debts, then the new business would contribute a bottom line profit increase. And so on.

Designing key ratios

There are any number of ratios which can be defined to measure the relationships between linked business events. However, only some of those ratios will be of enduring importance to the department or to the organization. Those key ratios will measure the fundamental activity carried on within that department. Before such key ratios can be selected, the objective or objectives of that department must be defined.

Normally, those objectives evolve through the planning process, as described earlier. They may be financial, such as profit targets (return on capital employed, or return on sales), or non-financial, such as improvement of quality (rate of rejects) or retention of staff (staff turnover). Any business unit will have a number of such objectives, and they can be ranked in order of relative importance so as to avoid conflict between them.

These objectives should be sub-divided within the organization in order to integrate with the corporate planning and short range budgeting approach previously discussed. Each part of the business should have a clearly defined objective to aim for which is visibly synchronized with the main objective of the organization. This leads to a number of basic principles of ratio selection:

- if possible, a manager should have few (one or two) key ratio indicators of his performance;
- a manager should have control over the factors which determine his performance;
- the factors which are linked through the key ratios should be logically interrelated.

Other aspects to remember when designing ratios are:

- *Consistency:* Clearly, it is important to maintain consistency between the numerator and the denominator of a ratio, and between the method of calculating a ratio and the standard with which it is being compared. For example, a commonly used ratio is one which relates debtors to sales. However, under normal accounting principles, United Kingdom debtors include Value Added Tax, whereas sales are usually quoted excluding that tax. Ratios derived from a straight calculation from published figures of two different companies where one was an exporter and the other served the home market would show a 15% difference which would be nothing at all to do with management performance!

- *Inflation:* If comparisons are being made of money values at different points in time, then the effects of inflation can be very significant. Those effects should be removed by using a suitable index to adjust values.

- *Averaging:* When relating profits, costs or sales to assets or capital, the figure for assets or capital should be an average of its values over the period to which the profits, costs or sales relate. Similarly, the number of staff who have left in a period should be related to the average number present during the same period, not to the number at either the beginning or the end of the period. In this way, the possible misleading effect of untypical fluctuations is avoided.

Key operating ratios

The most important operating ratio for nearly every business is return on shareholders' capital. Unfortunately, that immediately takes us into philosophical realms.

In private companies, where shares are not readily marketable and where the owners of the business are also the directors, the return consists of the directors' emoluments, payments into the directors' captive pension scheme and so on as well as any dividends. In this case, shareholders' capital might well be seen by the owners as the capital employed in the business (ie the balance sheet net assets).

On the other hand, in public companies, the shareholders are only in receipt of dividends plus such capital growth as their share may have. In this case, the capital value of their shares is nothing to do with the balance sheet assets of the company. That capital value is determined by the price of the share in the Stock Exchange market.

For the sake of simplicity, the return on capital employed key ratio will be defined as:

$$\frac{\text{Pre-tax profit}}{\text{Capital employed}}$$

This ratio reflects the fact that the business needs a certain level of assets (both infrastructure — long term related, and working capital — short term related) in order to make sales. It then has to extract profit from those sales. Thus this ratio can be expressed as the product of two separate activities:

$$\frac{\text{Pre-tax profit}}{\text{Capital employed}} = \frac{\text{Sales}}{\text{Capital employed}} \times \frac{\text{Pre-tax profit}}{\text{Sales}}$$

The relationship between sales and capital employed is termed asset turnover, and it measures the effectiveness with which assets are used to generate business. The relationship between pre-tax profit and sales is termed return on sales and shows the effectiveness with which business is converted to profits.

This relationship quite clearly shows the need for a business which is capital intensive to generate large margins on its sales. For example, shipbuilding or other heavy engineering companies make relatively few sales compared to their asset base, and hence need substantial profits on those sales to achieve a respectable level of profitability. On the other hand, commodity trading or food retailing companies need relatively little in the way of net margin on sales because the flow of sales through the capital employed is much greater. Statistics for a number of well known companies are given below:

Company	Sector	Asset turnover	Return on sales
Queens Moat Houses	Hotels	0.74×	10.3%
Marks & Spencer	Retailer	2.40×	9.4%
Trafalgar House	Conglomerate	4.92×	7.0%

The asset turnover and return on sales ratios can be exploded further in turn to yield their constituents.

Asset turnover

Ratios within this area relate to balance-sheet

management. Important relationships are:

- $\dfrac{\text{turnover}}{\text{fixed assets}}$ — measures the effectiveness with which fixed assets generate sales
- $\dfrac{\text{stock}}{\text{turnover}}$ — measures the level of business supported by the stockholding
- $\dfrac{\text{debtors}}{\text{turnover}}$ — measures the effectiveness of debtor management

Many other relationships are important, depending on the kind of business and the state of its operations. For most businesses, certain ratios will become very important but will then diminish in importance as problems are solved. The relationship between scrap rates (or rework) and throughput is a good example of a ratio which assumes great importance when new practices, product lines or machines are introduced, but then loses its pride of place as the new techniques or products become established.

Some of the other important capital management ratios are as follows:

- work-in-progress to total stock, turnover or cost of sales;
- actual production output to maximum production output;
- production shortages to buffer stock levels;
- rate of increase in suppliers' prices;
- suppliers' lead times;
- overdue orders placed on suppliers.

Return on sales

Ratios within this area relate to the effective management of expenses. Important relationships are:

- $\dfrac{\text{gross profit}}{\text{turnover}}$ — measures the level of variable cost versus fixed costs in a business
- $\dfrac{\text{selling expenses}}{\text{turnover}}$ — measures the effective cost to sell a unit of turnover
- $\dfrac{\text{turnover}}{\text{number of employees in the salesforce}}$ — measures the salesforce productivity

150

As with capital ratios, there may be a great many specific relationships which are important within a particular industry or business, but which are of no consequence elsewhere. Some of the more common ones are:

- growth in sales;
- growth of market share;
- mix of sales by segment and contribution by segment;
- proportion of sales of new products and contribution of new products;
- length of order book;
- proportion of items in bottom 20% of turnover;
- staff turnover and average cost per employee;
- output per employee.

For control purposes, each manager may need to purpose design his own key ratios, which will be valid for him (and perhaps for him only). Those key ratios may well only have a limited useful life, as business factors and the economic environment change.

Obtaining benchmarks

No ratio is meaningful in isolation. All ratios must be compared with a standard or benchmark to determine whether or not they are running at a satisfactory level. Normally, this standard is embodied in a budget derived from historical performance, but that is not the only source. Standards can be obtained from a variety of sources:

- *The firm's own past*

  This is perhaps the most frequently used standard. It has the advantage of comparing like with like: the products and the manufacturing and selling methods used are similar, and the methods by which the figures have been arrived at should be consistent over time.

  However, firstly, the standards achieved in the past by the firm may have been poor and to derive current standards from them may encourage a degree of complacency. Secondly, internal comparisons fail to take account of changes in the external economy. As a result, they may show an apparent improvement which may be the result more of a change in the economy than of a performance improvement on the part of the business.

● *The firm's assessment of the future (budgets)*

These are probably better standards of comparison than a firm's own past in that they should take into account the anticipated effect of changes in economic activity and the related impact on the industry concerned. They should also include the effect of inflation, and the impact of technological changes.

However, most budgets are heavily influenced by what has been achieved in the past. For that reason if a firm's performance in the past has been poor the budget may set a standard which is too low.

● *Other businesses*

Comparing performance with that of other businesses has a number of advantages. Firstly, if a reasonably wide and representative sample of other firms can be examined, it should be possible to ascertain standards of normal performance in the relevant industry. Secondly, it is possible to compare results over similar periods to ensure similar economic and technological conditions. Thirdly, a comparison of performance with what other firms have achieved avoids the subjective difficulties associated with budgets.

Such comparison can be done through some of the specialist firms which offer a service in this area. For example, the Centre for Interfirm Comparison collects performance information which is otherwise not publicly available, and publishes for its subscribers norms for industry segments. However, there is always some difficulty in performing such comparisons, since no two businesses are ever the same, and the results of any such study have to be treated as broad indicators of performance.

● *Work measurement*

Specific standards may be set in certain well defined areas. Time and motion study, activity sampling, build-up of a job from its basic components and estimating are techniques that can be used. They are used mostly on the production floor, but can be applied to clerical and managerial jobs as well. However, the less routine the task or content of the job, the more difficult it is to obtain a valid result.

Ratios are an excellent way of providing managers with simple, easy-to-understand targets. However, they are tools to use to meet particular needs, and they should be updated as those needs change.

Chapter 8

The financing proposal

Any new project or new business venture searching for funds whether from within the business organization or from outside sources has to justify or sell the proposed investment on grounds of return and feasibility. Such a justification involves a critical analytical process, of which the ultimate outcome should be a sound and well presented case for the finance required.

This Chapter will discuss only the approach to be taken with regard to the financial design of the funding package and its subsequent presentation. It will be assumed that financial appraisals have been performed along the lines already discussed in earlier Chapters, and that the result is an attractive business proposition which requires the provision of finance.

The reader should remember that whether internal or external, the potential provider of finance is concerned with his risk/reward ratio. As we saw in Chapter 3, different types of finance carry with them different degrees of risk and different rewards. For that reason the financial engineer needs to:

- assess the funds needed and the form that the funding should take;
- decide who to approach for funds;
- present the predicted returns available in a convincing way,

and blend all of these together into a sensible financing proposal which has due regard to the factors which are of interest to the prospective provider of finance.

1. Assessing funding needs

How much?

The objective is to assess the funds needed, not only in terms of how much is likely to be required but also in terms of the nature of the funding (debt versus equity) and the cost and repayment schedule which can be afforded.

There is nothing more embarrassing than to be unable to respond sensibly to the two fundamental questions which any potential provider of funds should ask at the commencement of discussions:

> "How much do you need and what for?"
> "How long do you want it for?"

From the point of view of the potential provider of funds the answers to those two questions will set the stage for all future discussions, since they define the possible extent of his commitment.

Determination of the funding requirement is not as simple as might appear, since the incidental funding effects of any new venture need to be included in the assessment. Sometimes these incidental effects are not at all obvious, such as the costs of training extra staff, or of financing higher stockholding or debtor levels. In addition, many businesses correctly compute their initial fixed assets and working capital finance, but fail to cater for the effects of growth and for the impact of initial losses.

The funding requirement for a self-contained business expansion, a new project or a totally new business is made up of money to cover capital expenditure, net working capital needs, and any initial operating costs which may not be covered by revenues (ie initial losses). Some of these initial costs are not recoverable in the event of failure of the venture. Other expenditure may be completely or partially recoverable from the proceeds of a liquidation. Therefore as a first step in the design of a funding proposal, the amount sought should be divided in such a way that it matches the amount of debt with the recoverable capital and ensures that risk capital which is potentially irrecoverable is covered by risk funding.

Any assessment of funding needs must include a forecast of the performance of the new venture. The flow of funds within a start-up business will be quite complex before self-funding is established. There will be substantial capital expense which will in turn combine with the working capital demands derived from the time-lags inherent within the transaction cycles of the business. There may be a need to pay for fixed overheads (such as payroll, rates or advertising) well before there are any earnings.

Because of the complex interplay of all these factors, the forecast should look far enough ahead to enable the venture to demonstrate that it has or could reach self-sufficient maturity — that is to say, by the end of the projected period the new venture should be demonstrably paying its way.

It may be that this forecast shows that there will be a period of initial losses before the business breaks even and commences to recover lost ground. If so, the second stage of funding design is to ensure that the business is a bankable proposition at the predicted point of peak losses. It is an empirical rule that the greatest strain on funds never comes at the date of opening or commencement of a new venture. The strain always comes a little later — perhaps three to six months on, or even after a year. The reason is simple. Management are typically spending now to generate future revenues. There is also a general tendency to "buy business", ie to take on business which generates little or no profit in order to enter new markets. Unfortunately, this has the effect of transforming liquid cash into illiquid debtors and stock without any cash benefit to the business. In combination with the other great demands that are made on resources at that time these perfectly understandable business stratagems can prove fatal.

This peaking of demands on cash are illustrated below:

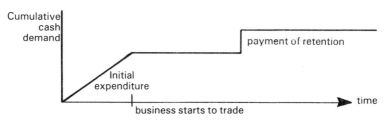

Typical capital expenditure pattern of a new business

Typical working capital needs of a new business

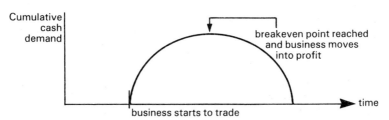

Typical initial losses (initial excess of fixed overheads over contribution)

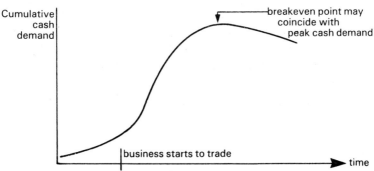

Total funding needs showing the sharp peak experienced well after trading has commenced

This graph shows the way the sum total of capital expenditure, working capital needs and losses peaks well after commencement of trade, perhaps at about the time the business has just "turned the corner". Experience proves that at that point the business could very easily be running just in excess of its agreed overdraft limit. If at that time the bank manager calls for accounts they will show that much of the owners' initial capital has been eaten up by losses. It is possible that the bank will consider that at that point its interest is best served by appointing a receiver.

What kind?

The key to avoiding receivership is to design correctly the capital structure and borrowing facilities of a new business. In other words, the capital structure at the outset has to be capable of sustaining the impact of those initial losses and the financing arrangements have to provide sufficient cash to cover for the inevitable slippage. There has to be sufficient risk money in the enterprise to convince the bank that at its worst point the business will still survive.

Consider the following example:

Microx Electro Limited is a new company formed to manufacture and market the Microx electromagnetic field controller. Initial fixed asset expenditure is likely to amount to £200,000, working capital needs are about £80,000, and it is expected that due to market development costs and the general start-up sales lag, at the conclusion of the first six months' trading the business will have lost £110,000. However, thereafter the business should be profitable. The owners are able to invest £140,000 of their own money, but are unwilling to sell any equity to raise further capital.

The external funding needed is as follows:

Fixed assets	200,000
Working capital	80,000
	280,000
Less: owners' funds	(140,000)
External funding need	140,000

All too often this sort of funding need is dealt with by borrowing on an overdraft facility of £140,000. If that is done, then after six months the balance sheet of the business looks as follows:

Fixed assets	200,000
Working capital	(30,000)
	170,000
Less: overdraft	(140,000)
Net assets	30,000
Share capital	140,000
Losses	(110,000)
Shareholders' funds	30,000

There is an immediate and serious problem. Working capital has gone negative probably because suppliers (creditors) have not been paid. Furthermore, they cannot be paid since the bank overdraft is at its limit. The bank will certainly not increase facilities, since gearing is now very high with shareholders' funds of £30,000 as against bank debt of £140,000. Sooner or later either the bank or the creditors will call in the receiver.

Contrast the position had the company sold some of its shares off to outsiders in order to secure the funding. Enough equity would need to be sold to raise sufficient funds to present the bank with a tolerable position at the worst point. In other words, at the six month stage the gearing should have been about 1 : 1 at most. This would have been the case if the company had raised £55,000 of equity (risk) money.

The six month balance sheet would be as follows:

Fixed assets	200,000
Working capital	(30,000)
	170,000
Less: overdraft	(85,000)
Net assets	85,000
Share capital — owners	140,000
Share capital — other	55,000
Losses	(110,000)
Shareholders' funds	85,000

The gearing is now at a satisfactory level of £85,000 of shareholders' funds to £85,000 of borrowings, and there is plenty of room left in the overdraft. True, the shareholders have sold some element of their ownership of the company, but at least there is still a viable business entity in existence.

The extra funding obtained by the sale of equity is risk money. It shares the same risks as the owners of the business, but also shares in the rewards in the same way as the owners do.

In addition to this basic principle of funding to permit a business to survive its initial losses, the other major question relates to the matching of cash generation and repayment of indebtedness. The fixed assets and the working capital of any business need to be financed from sources which match their respective long and short term nature.

We have already reviewed the principal commercial sources of funds in Chapter 3. All the potential sources of finance available to a business are summarised below:

- *equity,* which is the contribution to the funds of a business by the owners of that business. The rewards of equity ownership are a right to all of the profits and to the net assets of the business. However, the attendant risk is that the equity owners are last in the pay-out queue if the business has to cease trading for any reason.

- *term loans,* which bear interest and which are normally secured and repayable by fixed instalments over a number of years. The lenders' reward is the interest rate which they charge regardless of the level of profitability of the business. The lenders' risk is usually minimised because the loan is well secured.

- *overdrafts,* which bear interest and which are normally secured but which are repayable on demand. Risks and rewards looked for by the providers of overdrafts are similar to those required by long term lenders.

- *government grants and "soft" loans,* eligibility for which can depend on industry sector, geographical location or other factors. In general, the rewards for such assistance may relate to social paybacks such as job creation or other requisites, which if not fulfilled can result in clawback of the assistance.

- *creditors and advance payments* from customers, which as previously discussed in Chapter 5 can provide some level of free finance but which if abused can imperil the business.

The funding sources described have different characteristics, as do the business assets which are being funded. The funding of a business or of a project should be engineered or designed in such a way that the yield characteristics of the enterprise match the repayment and servicing characteristics of the funding.

For example, fixed assets like plant, machinery and buildings have relatively long useful lives. By their nature, they provide ready security for purposes of borrowing. The cash generated over the lifetime of a machine can match and pay off the associated borrowing and interest over a number of years. For that reason, term loans and leasing provide an excellent funding medium for fixed asset purchases. Further, in many instances the whole of the capital finance required may be fundable through external borrowing.

The funding requirements of working capital are rather different. The debtors, creditors and stock that make up working capital are subjected to a process of continuous transformation which liquidates (ie encashes) each individual item only to create more as the capital circulates rapidly and continually within the transaction cycle of the business. Short term net assets of this kind can be validly funded by equivalent short term overdraft borrowings. However, because of the risks involved with debtors (the possibility of bad debts) and with stocks (deterioration, obsolescence and warranty costs) it is generally imprudent to borrow all of the working capital requirements of a business.

Finally, the funding of risky enterprises which are large in relation to the size of an existing business (like the costs of entering a major new market or of developing a promising new product to commercial production) should be financed by risk money, ie equity. If the project is successful, then the old and the new equity holders win hands down. If the project is unsuccessful, then they all lose. However, if finance is structured this way, at least the business should survive. It may not survive if the money is borrowed.

2. Deciding whom to approach

The objective here is to decide who to approach for the funds, the nature of their interest, how to convince them to participate and how to pay them off or buy them out eventually. In this context it is important to understand the perspectives of the providers of funds:

- Banks look for the ability of the business to service the interest cost and to repay the amount borrowed assuming that the business runs normally. Thus they will look at cash flow projections and profit and loss accounts. They will also be concerned about the vulnerability of the business to economic fluctuations. Thus they will assess balance sheet and profit and loss gearing. Finally, they will consider the ability of the business to pay back the amounts borrowed were it to cease trading. Therefore, they will assess security.

- Venture capital funds make risk investments because they accept that potentially high rewards must be matched by commensurate risks. Consequently, they look for high growth rates and are less concerned about income (ie dividends). However, they will always look for a way to realise their investment. For these reasons, venture capital funds will be concerned with the commercial soundness of the proposition (that is to say, the market opportunity, the product and the quality of the management), returns in terms of future growth and the eventual realisation of their investment.

At one extreme, we may consider a well established textile company with little or no borrowing requiring the funding of a major renewal of its finishing machinery. The utilisation of the machinery is predictable and earnings should well cover interest and cash generation will cover repayments. Security is available and there is no reason to suppose that this would not prove to be an eminently suitable proposal for a long term loan from a bank.

At the other extreme, a brand new United Kingdom-based manufacturer of software wishes to enter the North American market. His costs will be large in relation to his capital base but the market potential and the financial returns are enormous. Almost certainly, this is not a bankable proposition, but a venture capital fund may well be very interested.

There are a great number of different types of organisation which provide funds of one kind or another. Each has a different approach and different criteria and requirements. It is beyond the scope of this book to list these organisations, but lists are from time to time printed in the *Investors' Chronicle* and in other publications, and suitable organisations may be recommended by firms of accountants. Lists can also be obtained through the British Venture Capital Association, 1 Surrey Street, London WC2.

3. Predicting and presenting the returns available

Most providers of funds see themselves only partly as investing in a business opportunity. Mostly, they see themselves as investing in management's ability to exploit that opportunity.

Those potential providers of funds need to be convinced that the proposition constitutes sound lending or a worthwhile investment. In other words, they need to be shown that management have established commercial viability:

- researched and thought the venture through thoroughly;
- mapped out what to do and how and when to do it;
- reasonably assessed financing needs and likely returns.

Commercial viability can best be demonstrated by means of a business plan. The business plan is much more than a forecast of the financial performance of a project. It is a comprehensive formulation of the non-financial and financial goals of the project, and of the detailed steps to be taken in achieving them. It is as much a test of management as it is a test of the business opportunity!

The detailed accent and slant of the business plan will depend on the audience it intends to address, and whether it is internal or external. However, for any significant new project it should always contain:

- *summary*
  - how much is wanted and what will be done with it;
  - what form the funding is to take, and how long it is required for;
  - the prospective reward for the provider;

- *the business opportunity*
  - the total potential market and its characteristics
  - marketing, and how the company will achieve its market share
  - the competition and their likely reaction
  - details of the product or services
  - the factors which differentiate the product from the competition
  - production and production plan;

- *the management and staff*
  - their role in the new operation
  - previous experience and qualifications
  - staff numbers required;

- *financial performance*
  - history of the company
  - current balance sheet and profit and loss
  - projected profit and loss, cash flow and balance sheets, showing peak borrowing requirements and pattern of returns
  - risk factors, their possible effect and steps taken to mitigate them;

- *statement of funding requirements*
  - funds already available

- amount of funds needed and their proposed form
- security available (if applicable)
- the proposed exit route for the investor.

The above is a general list and each application must be individually tailored to ensure that it appropriately addresses the proposed audience and does justice to the business opportunity.

Needless to say, such a document can be usefully used internally within the business as an integral part of the planning process.

Chapter 9

Published accounts

We have seen that the limited liability company is a privileged entity, in that it has its own legal existence which is distinct and separate from that of its shareholders. As a consequence, it can raise capital by way of sale of shares in itself while restricting the commitment of its shareholders to a defined amount. Further, it can appoint officers to conduct its affairs, and those officers need not be themselves shareholders. These legal privileges and powers make the limited liability company a flexible and powerful vehicle for combining the skills of individuals with managerial talent but no capital with the capital funding capability of others.

This potential ability to separate the provision of capital from day-to-day management is best illustrated by a simple structural model of a limited liability company:

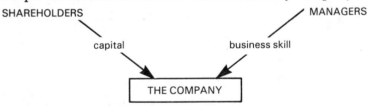

However, fundamental issues of control arise if the providers of capital (who are, after all, the owners of the business) are no longer the managers of the business enterprise, but are instead relegated to a relatively passive and perhaps remote role. Those issues are:

- how should the managers report to the shareholders the results of their stewardship?

- how can the shareholders be sure of the accuracy and truthfulness of the managers' reports?

History has evolved the answer to these questions in the form of annual audited accounts, and the rules which govern their production are enshrined in legislation and in guidelines issued by the professional accounting institutes. These statutory accounts are usually referred to as published accounts, since they must be filed at Companies House, where they are available for inspection by any member of the public. They are important, because they can provide to the informed outsider a great deal of information about the performance of a business.

1. The objectives of published accounts

The original straightforward purpose of publishing annual audited accounts was to report to the existing shareholders the state of affairs of the business which they owned. The underlying principle was that the directors of the business who ran it on behalf of the remote owners (the shareholders) would prepare an annual accounting to those owners. That accounting would be checked on behalf of the shareholders by independent, expert outsiders (the auditors), who would report to the shareholders alongside the directors. Thus was introduced a control over the performance of the directors.

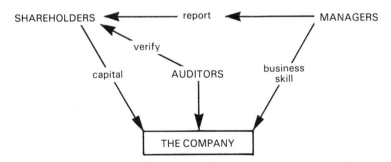

The shareholders' interest in the annual accounts was always clear cut and easy to define. They were interested principally in the wealth or value of their business and in their share of it, and in the ability of the business to continue to pay or to increase dividends.

However, since published accounts were available for inspection on the public file, other interested parties soon came to realise the usefulness of published financial information about individual businesses. We have already seen in Chapter 1 that a wide body of individuals and organisations may use published accounts:

- potential investors, to determine whether they should invest;
- providers of funds, such as banks, to determine permissible levels of funding, compliance with loan covenants, etc;
- employees, to formulate wage claims, to determine employer performance and to judge security of employment;
- creditors, to evaluate risk of non-recovery of credit extended;
- customers, to determine security of supply;
- competitors, to evaluate strengths and weaknesses, and to compare performance;
- the Inland Revenue, as part of the tax collection process;
- potential acquirors, regulatory bodies, Trade Unions etc.

Each of these sets of users is interested in one particular aspect of a company's financial performance. For example, the prospective investor may be interested principally in the prospects for future growth and dividends (as assessed against a backcloth of historical performance); the bank may be interested in gearing and security cover and competitors may want to assess sales and profit performance in relation to assets employed. Thus published accounts have become an important source of different information to a great many different users.

Published accounts attempt to meet the information needs of these user groups in three ways:

- by showing an overall "true and fair" view of the state of affairs of the business;

- by adopting certain standards of presentation and consistency of accounting treatment;
- by disclosing additional information relevant to the needs of specific user groups.

True and fair view

By law, the directors of a limited liability company are required to present published accounts which show a true and fair view. In turn, the auditors are required to report on those accounts to the shareholders, and state whether in their opinion those accounts show a "true and fair view".

However, there is no precise definition of what "true and fair view" means. Indeed, it is easier to attempt to define that phrase in negative terms. Published accounts will not present a true and fair view if:

- they contain inaccurate or misleading information. This is not just a matter of overstated profit or blatant lies. Very often the misstatement can be rather more subtle. The essential test is whether the inaccuracy will change the views of user groups. For example, consider the common situation of a loan repayable over 5 years under normal conditions but repayable on demand at the bank's option in the event of breach of a loan covenant. If the covenant is breached, the loan should be classified as a current liability in the published accounts, which may show the company as having much greater current liabilities than current assets. There may be a great temptation to continue to treat the loan as long term, since to reflect the actual state of affairs might encourage suppliers to restrict credit;

- they omit information without which the accounts do not present a comprehensive portrayal of the business. For example, a company may have entered into contractual arrangements to buy forward its raw materials requirements under a guaranteed call-off schedule in return for a price reduction. Clearly, a business which has entered into such an arrangement for the next year is in a different position from one (which may be identical in all other respects) which has not. This kind of arrangement alters the operating risks

- they fail to follow accepted practice without good reason. The major issue here is consistency, and the need to follow what is commonly accepted and expected by accountants, business people, investors and the like. Accepted good practice is set out in guidelines published by the accountancy institutes (see Appendix 1), and a breach of those guidelines without cause would prejudice the true and fair view;

- there is a significant uncertainty or lack of information. For example, if the company is being sued and it is not possible to tell how the law-suit will be resolved or what the quantum of damages might be. Or, the realisability might not be known of large amounts of foreign currency locked up in a foreign country due to exchange controls.

In summary, accounts will not present a "true and fair view" unless the information that they contain is adequate in quantity and quality to satisfy the reasonable expectations of the user groups involved. Note too that the requirement to present a true and fair view is global in nature. There is no guarantee that the accounts are correct, or that individual items within the accounts are precisely right. Indeed, given the assumptions and conventions that go into preparing a set of published accounts it is difficult to envisage that any such guarantee could be given. The best we get is that the net profit and the net worth as set out are about right under certain specific conditions.

Standards of presentation and consistency of accounting treatment

One of the difficulties encountered by analysts when reviewing and comparing the results of different companies is that the accounting assumptions made by them and embodied within their published accounts can be materially different. For example, buildings may be depreciated over periods ranging from 30 years to 100 years or more. Machinery may be written off over 3 years or over 20. As a consequence, the results of the companies being compared may appear to be very different when in fact they are not.

The accounting institutes have published guidelines in an effort to improve the consistency of treatment, and in order to set out formally the generally accepted view of what constitutes best practice. Those guidelines are termed SSAPs — *Statements of Standard Accounting Practice*. Each SSAP addresses one topic. At the time of writing there are twenty-one topics which have been addressed in this way, ranging from the calculation of earnings per share to the accounting treatment of mergers. These SSAPs set out the acceptable range of assumptions and conventions which may be applied to specific areas of business activity in different circumstances (see Appendix 1).

Clearly, the establishment of guidelines imposes some restrictions on the diversity of accounting treatment which might otherwise be used. Furthermore, one of the SSAPs (SSAP2) requires that the actual accounting policies adopted by the business have to be set out as an integral part of the published accounts, thus allowing the users to adjust for any inconsistencies between the companies being compared.

Disclosure of additional information relevant to the needs of specific user groups

In addition to the requirement for a "true and fair view" to be presented by the published accounts, there are certain specific provisions contained in the legislation which relate to disclosure of information. Those provisions deal with units of information of special interest to particular user groups. For example, details of action taken by the company to maintain employee involvement and a note of the company's policy on employment of disabled persons have to be given in the directors' report. Details of future capital commitments have to be set out in the notes to the accounts, and so forth. In this way some of the extra information needs of user groups are met.

In recent years there has been a considerable growth in the number of companies which publish a special annual financial report purely for the use of their employees. There is no statutory requirement to produce such a document, but there is much to be gained by communicating regularly and openly with the workforce.

2. The legislation

The law which governs the financial reporting requirements for limited liability companies is set out in the Companies Act 1985. Among other matters, that law deals with:

- financial reporting; and
- audit requirements.

Financial reporting

Firstly, it is the Companies Act which obliges the directors to report annually to the shareholders. From an accounting point of view there is no special logic in having annual accounts. Indeed, the economic cycle of many businesses spans years rather than months, and the selection of an annual date for reporting is highly artificial. It could be argued that for many other businesses, annual reporting is insufficient and that reports should be made more frequently.

Secondly, the Act specifies the format of the accounts which the directors are to produce, the information to be disclosed, the basic accounting policies to be adopted and the asset valuation rules to be used. The contents must include:

- a review of the company's activities and profits, including segment information, likely future prospects and post-balance sheet date events, dividends and directors' interests;
- a summary of the important accounting policies adopted and the basis of preparation of the accounts;
- comprehensive information concerning fixed assets, investments, stock, liabilities, commitments, capital and reserves.

Finally, the Act sets out the rules relating to the public filing of published accounts. The responsibility for filing annual audited accounts rests with the directors (who are also primarily responsible for the accuracy of the information contained within the accounts). Those accounts must be filed at Companies House as follows:

- public limited company (plc)—within 7 months of the year-end. (However, the Stock Exchange requires results for quoted companies to be announced within six months of their year end),
- private limited company—within 10 months of the year-end.

A further three month extension is added to these deadlines for companies with overseas subsidiaries.

The Act relaxes public disclosure rules for small companies, and permits them to file abridged accounts which consist of a balance sheet and abbreviated notes.

Audit requirements

Audited accounts are required for all limited companies incorporated in the United Kingdom. Auditors are the representatives of the shareholders and so must be appointed by them at the Annual General Meeting (AGM), and hold office until the next AGM. However, they can be removed by the shareholders at any time.

The auditor is not legally obliged to examine and report on any matter other than those contained within a set of accounts as defined by the Act. However, if certain information is not set out within the accounts, he must give it himself if he is able so to do. This applies, for example, to details of loans to directors and directors' emoluments.

3. The components of a set of published accounts

A set of statutory accounts must include the following elements:

- Directors' report
- Auditors' report
- Balance Sheet
- Profit and loss account
- Funds flow statement
- Details of accounting policies
- Notes to accounts.

Directors' report

By law, the directors' report must contain a review of the results of trade for the year and an indication of prospects for the future as well as details of any dividends which may be proposed. Certain other specific information must also be included. The directors' report is often turned into a public relations exercise, but nevertheless can reveal a good deal in quantitative terms about the strategy and performance of a business.

Auditors' report

The auditors report whether or not, in their view, the accounts present a true and fair view. Their report will most probably be unqualified. However, on those occasions where a qualification exists, careful reading of the report is indicated.

A "subject to" qualification indicates that a significant uncertainty exists which, when clarified or resolved, will most probably have a material impact on the company. Details of the uncertainty will be described most probably in the notes to the accounts. An example of such an uncertainty might be a substantial law suit, the outcome of which cannot be assessed.

An "except for" qualification indicates that the auditors were unable to agree with the accounting treatment adopted by the directors for a specific item in the accounts. For example, a disagreement might arise over the realisability of expenses incurred in order to develop a market. The directors may consider that those expenses are an asset, fully recoverable against the future profits to be derived from that market, whereas the auditors may be of the view that there is insufficient evidence to support recoverability and that those expenses should not be treated as an asset but as an immediate expense. If there are any such disagreements, details will be set out in the auditors' report or elsewhere within the accounts.

Balance sheet

As with any balance sheet, the statutory balance sheet is a snapshot of the affairs of the company at its year end. However, its layout and presentation must conform to an approved statutory format. In its most common format, one side of the statutory balance sheet shows the sources of capital and where they originate from:

- supplied by the shareholders;
- retained from the profits of the business.

The other side shows the net assets which are being funded by the capital at one specific point in time, classified under certain specific headings as required by law:

- *fixed assets:* those assets held for use in the business rather than for resale or conversion into cash;
- *current assets:* circulating assets held for resale or conversion into cash;
- *current liabilities:* amounts owing by the business which will become due for payment in the 12 months following the balance sheet date;
- *long-term liabilities:* amounts owing but due for payment more than 12 months after the balance sheet date.

Profit and loss account

The statutory profit and loss account must show the results of operations for the current year, any dividends paid and proposed and transfers to or from reserves, if any. In that way it links the prior year statutory balance sheet to the current year balance sheet.

Funds flow statement

The funds flow statement is not a statutory requirement. It is a requirement imposed by the SSAPs issued by the accounting institutes. It shows the sources and use of funds over the year as a whole. Thus it links the profit and loss account and the individual components of the prior year balance sheet to those of the current year.

Accounting policies

This section of the accounts sets out the accounting policies which have been used in preparing the accounts. We have already seen the importance of understanding them, particularly if the reader wants to compare the performance of different companies. Differences between accounting policies (eg on depreciation rates) can distort comparison and lead to incorrect conclusions.

Notes to accounts

These provide additional disclosure details and any required breakdown of balance sheet and profit and loss captions.

4. Accounting conventions

Published accounts are ultimately a product of the application of accounting conventions and the exercise of professional judgement. Existing rules and guidelines allow considerable scope for the use of different accounting conventions, leading to the possibility of disparate reporting even for similar businesses. For this reason, financial statements cannot be validly analysed without understanding the nature of the accounting conventions and estimates used in their preparation.

It should also be remembered that the published accounts are aimed principally at the shareholders, and as such, the auditors' assurance that those accounts are "true and fair" refers only to the global picture portrayed by them specifically under "going-concern" conditions.

Details of the principal specific conventions used must be set out in each set of accounts, usually under a separate heading. The "going-concern" assumption is fundamental to any set of accounts. A list of the other general implied assumptions and uncertainties that exist within most sets of published accounts is given below:

Fixed assets

For most companies, fixed assets consist of two very different types of tangible property. Firstly, businesses may own land and buildings. Secondly, nearly all businesses have plant, machinery, fixtures and fittings. The value of fixed assets, which in many companies can be very substantial indeed, affects the net assets of the business; the depreciation charged on those assets can be a large profit and loss burden.

Land and buildings are typically recorded in the accounts at original cost less depreciation. If that is the case (and depending on when it was bought) the current value may be significantly in excess of the book value. More rarely, land and buildings may have been revalued, in which case the books will probably show a more accurate picture. However, any valuation will have been done on an existing use basis. If the assets ever came up for sale for alternative use the achieved value could be much lower or much greater than the value to the business.

Plant, machinery and fixtures and fittings are also recorded at cost less depreciation. Depreciation is provided so as to write off those assets to their residual value over their useful lifetimes. However, we all know that in terms of resale value, new cars, computers and office furniture are all worth at best half of what we paid for them an instant after purchase.

So the real value of fixed assets will be different from the balance sheet net assets of the business as calculated under accounting conventions, since land and buildings may be shown in the books at less than their value in the real world, whereas plant and machinery will most probably be shown at more than their real value.

Further, from the point of view of the profit and loss account, a business which has revalued its factory buildings will have to levy a larger depreciation charge than one which has not. So will a business which believes that its premises have a useful life of 25 years as compared to a business which occupies similar premises but which thinks that they will last for 50 years.

Thus, there is much room for diversity and difference of treatment; and the financial effect of the differences can be very marked since for many businesses the value of fixed assets is substantial.

Stock

Accounting conventions require that stock be recorded in the books at cost, or the value it will fetch when sold, whichever is lower. However, even in the simplest business, the definition of what constitutes cost may be difficult.

For example, consider a retailing business which has in stock one white shirt which cost £4.00. A second identical shirt is purchased by the business for £5.00. Then, one of the shirts is sold for £7.00. What is the cost of the remaining shirt, and what profit has the business made in that transaction?

The correct answer is that it depends on what flow assumption you use to define cost. If you assume that the last physical receipt was the one sold, the transaction profit is £2.00 and the residual stock cost is £4.00. This cost flow assumption is called LIFO (last-in, first-out). However, if you assume that the first physical receipt was the one sold, then the transaction profit is £3.00 and the residual stock cost is £5.00. This cost flow assumption is called FIFO (first-in, first-out). An alternative treatment is to average the cost of purchases, in which case the transaction profit would be £2.50 and the residual stock cost would be £4.50. (See also Chapter 2, where there is another example of stock valuation.)

It is apparent that the cost flow assumption adopted could have a significant effect on the reported profit, particularly at a time when prices are changing rapidly. Consequently, the assumption used has to be set out in the notes to the published accounts. FIFO is the basis most commonly adopted in United Kingdom accounts.

As a further complication, in most manufacturing businesses stock is a mixture of raw materials, work-in-progress and finished goods. The cost of raw materials can be established by reference to the purchase price (using a cost flow assumption if necessary). However, both work-in-progress and finished goods have probably been worked on by the labour force, and have occupied some of the factory's capacity to produce. As a result, both of these elements of stock have to have added to their raw material constituent the cost of the labour expended on them and some portion of the factory overheads. The amounts to be added are very often impossible to define precisely, and global estimates may have to be used.

Finally, there is the question of realisability. If stock is obsolete, through changes in fashion or technology, deteriorated, or physically damaged it may not even command its cost price. In that case it needs to be recorded in the books at the estimated realisable value, net of selling expenses.

All of these factors combine to make the valuation of stock an inexact science, particularly if the company concerned is in an industry where prices or technology are changing rapidly.

Debtors

Merged within the debtors figure in most published accounts will be two very different types of business asset. For most businesses, debtors consist not only of straightforward money receivable from customers (ie trade debtors), but also of money paid for future benefits (prepayments), and sundry other items (such as advance corporation tax). Trade debtors will in due course be transformed into cash inflows. Prepayments will not give rise directly to future cash inflows, since they arise as a result of the application of accounting convention and are in effect deferrals of expenditure.

Trade debtors themselves may not represent future cash inflows exactly. If there are foreign currency debtors included in those balances, they will have been translated into sterling at the rates of exchange ruling at the date of the balance sheet. The debt may be paid much later in the denominating foreign currency, but if the rate of exchange has changed, the sterling amount received could be different to that recorded at the balance sheet date. Furthermore, the incidence of bad debts could reduce the amounts realised from debtors.

Cash

Even old-fashioned cash is subject to some degree of uncertainty. Cash occasionally includes short-term deposits and investments which can be turned quickly into cash. but investments sometimes lose value unexpectedly, and in 1973, at the time of the secondary banking crisis, there were many businesses which realised less than the full amount of investments placed with those banks.

Cash held in foreign currency is subject to the same exchange rate variations and exposures as the debtors denominated in foreign currency. Furthermore, if money is held abroad, foreign exchange controls in certain countries may effectively freeze the cash in the country where it is held, so that it can only be used to pay local bills.

Current liabilities

The money owed by businesses falls into a number of categories. There are amounts owed for goods and services supplied to the business. There is funding for business operations provided by the bank through the medium of an overdraft, and there are taxes payable. In some businesses, for example, holiday operators, there are also deposits paid by customers for goods or services to be provided by the business.

There is uncertainty here too. Some of these amounts may be estimates, or subject to exchange rate fluctuation.

Others may have ill-defined repayment dates: for example, overdrafts are repayable on demand, but in practice may constitute permanent finance for many stable businesses.

Long term liabilities

Long term liabilities contain by far the greatest medley of items of different accounting nature. Here are classified long term loans (or that portion of loans due in over one year), long term loan equivalents such as the notional repayments of principal due under finance lease agrecments, deferred taxation and other amounts due after more than one year from the balance sheet date.

In particular, deferred taxation is an amalgamation of estimates. It represents the amount of taxation ultimately payable but currently deferred by reason of tax allowances. The accuracy (and adequacy) of the deferred tax provision depends on the accuracy with which future rates of capital expenditure and future fiscal regimes can be predicted. For example, most companies had to provide (charge an extra amount to the profit and loss account) for extra deferred taxation when the Chancellor recently changed the rules on capital allowances.

The details of current generally accepted accounting principles are set out within The Statements of Standard Accounting Practice (SSAPs). The current SSAPs are listed in Appendix 1.

5. Analysing published accounts

We have already discussed the use within a business of ratios to measure performance. Ratio analysis can also be used very effectively to gain insights into the comparative performance of other businesses, such as competitors, suppliers, or customers.

Whereas management ratios are designed principally to pinpoint sensitive areas which require close scrutiny and control, the ratio analysis of published accounts has as its objective the dissection of the subject company into its financial structure with the aim of identifying financial strengths and weaknesses. For that reason, logical relationships between the constituents of published accounts can be termed structural ratios.

The principle of ratio design is the same as that used for management accounting. Two causally linked pieces of information (normally measured in financial terms) are brought together to create a dimensionless reference number which can be used to measure trends between periods and to compare different businesses. The figures can both be taken from the balance sheet, the profit and loss, or one may be taken from each.

The structural ratios to be used will be determined by the nature and purpose of the analyst. For example, important factors which will need to be measured under different circumstances will include:

- *analysis of competitor performance*
    - sales in relation to factors which limit sales (eg fixed assets, employees or stocks)
    - gross profit achieved on sales
    - operating profit achieved on sales
    - level of working capital required to support sales

- *analysis of supplier or customer financial stability*
    - level of borrowed capital as compared to shareholders' equity
    - cash generation compared to cash outflows
    - trends of operating profit to sales
    - trends of net cash flows as compared to sales
    - ratio of current liabilities to current assets
    - degree to which interest charges are covered by operating profit
    - creditors as a proportion of total purchases

- *analysis of investment potential*
    - relationship between earnings and share price
    - relationship between dividends and share price
    - extent to which the share price is underpinned by underlying asset value.

Whatever the analytical job to be performed, an understanding of the constituents of the financial statements which are to be analysed is essential. That is because it is important to ensure that comparisons which are to be made between different companies are done on a comparable basis. For that reason, the analytical process entails three steps:

- adjustment
- separation
- analysis.

Adjustment

This process ensures that the data being used for analysis is comparable and consistent in terms of the underlying accounting assumptions and conventions.

The principal adjustment which is nearly always necessary is the restatement of fixed assets to current value. Because of the significance of fixed assets to most businesses it is useful to measure the effectiveness of use of these assets. However, we have already seen that published accounts contain a collection of historical costs relating to the original cost of fixed assets. Accordingly, an estimate of current value has to be made, and the Companies Act requires disclosure of significant differences between the book and actual value of land and buildings for this and similar purposes.

Other adjustments might need to be made in respect of depreciation rates and other dissimilarities in accounting policies. The accounting policies section of the published accounts should be read with care to identify areas of divergence.

Separation

The net profits of a business attributable to shareholders are calculated after deduction of taxation and interest. Taxation costs are principally a function of fiscal regimes, and interest cost is a function of the capital structuring of a business. From a shareholder's point of view they are important costs and form an integral part of the costs of the return generated by the business, but the analyst must separate them and assess them in different ways.

Operating profit must be compared with operating assets and operating capital. Thus for purposes of analysis interest expense or income should be removed along with the related borrowings or deposits. Financing costs can be compared with borrowed capital, if desired. Any other non-business items, such as quoted or unquoted investments should be removed, along with the related income or losses.

Taxation is generally not considered in the performance analysis process, on the basis that all companies are equally affected. However, it would certainly have to be considered by an international investor, or in the case when performance issues were secondary because survival was uncertain.

Analysis

We have earlier seen that the analytical process depends to some extent on the analyst's brief. Broadly speaking, ratios may be broken down into three major areas:

- operating ratios, which measure internal performance;
- financial ratios, which measure cash position and financial capacity;
- investor ratios, which measure external performance.

Within each of these divisions is a number of important ratios which can serve as a starting point for any detailed analytical process:

Operating ratios

Net profit/sales — return on sales %, most often used for performance comparison purposes

Net profit/net assets	— return on capital employed %, most often used as a measure of return available from alternatives
Gross profit/sales	— enables a broad estimate to be made of the effect of an increase in sales on operating profit, and measures production efficiency
Turnover/fixed assets	— measures effectiveness of use of fixed assets
Stock turnover (Cost of sales/Stock)	— measures effectiveness of stock management
Debtor turnover (Sales/Debtors)	— measures effectiveness of debtor management
Output per employee	— measures productivity

Financial ratios

Current ratio (current assets/current liabilities)	— measures the ability of a business to pay its bills where stock is risk-free
Quick ratio (current assets less stock/current liabilities)	— measures the liquidity of a business where stock is not quickly and easily saleable
Gearing (gross borrowings/shareholders' funds)	— measures company's dependence on external sources of funds and borrowing capacity
Interest cover (profit before interest and taxation/internal cost)	— measures the depth of coverage for committed interest

Investor ratios

| Earnings per share (net profit after tax/ no. of ordinary shares in issue) | — measures maximum earnings available to be dividended per share |
| Price/earnings (market price/earnings per share) | — value placed on company by the market place |

185

Dividend yield (gross dividend/share price)	— measures the running yield available to investors
Dividend cover (earnings/dividends)	— measures the depth of coverage for the dividend
Asset cover (net assets/number of ordinary shares in issue)	— measures tangible value of shares

More detailed ratios can be developed to investigate and compare areas of specific interest.

Chapter 10

Corporate finance

Corporate finance is a broad and reasonably non-specific term which covers dealings on the Stock Exchange, provision of finance for private companies, mergers, acquisitions and management buy-outs.

1. The Stock Exchange

The Stock Exchange is a highly sophisticated market where the commodity being traded is stocks and shares. As with any market, prices fluctuate up and down, depending on the state of the economy, market sentiment and the performance of individual companies.

It might be argued that there exist two different markets on the Stock Exchange:

- the market in new shares floated on the Stock Exchange. This market enables Government and industry to raise capital;

- the aftermarket market in second-hand shares traded between investors, which has no direct immediate impact on the company which originally issued those shares, but which is directly relevant to the ability of that company to obtain further capital at reasonable cost from the Stock Exchange.

Upon entering the market, every quoted public company covenants with the Stock Exchange that it will abide by certain standards of behaviour, relating principally to disclosure of information to the market and accountability to the shareholders. In addition, it is bound by the Rules of The Panel on Takeovers and Mergers.

New issues

To enter the market, the company has to find a stock-broker who is prepared to sponsor entry either himself, or in conjunction with a merchant bank (an issuing house). The sponsor will verify that the company is suitable for entering public life by reviewing its financial position, future prospects, the quality of its management and its ability to be accountable to its public shareholders. The mechanisms of entry have already been discussed in Chapter 3.

Raising further capital

A rights issue involves the allotment of additional shares to existing shareholders for cash. The existing share-holders are effectively given the opportunity to buy new shares *pro rata* to their shareholding, normally at a slight discount from market price. This means that the rights themselves may have a value, which is the difference between the selling price asked for by the company and the price at which shares can be bought in the market.

In such an issue shareholders may either take up their rights, sell their rights, or do nothing (in which case their rights are normally sold for them).

From the company's point of view, the objective of a rights issue is to raise funds to finance expansion, repay borrowings or to make acquisitions. The company will try to maximise the price of the new shares, while at the same time attempting to make that price sufficiently attractive to ensure that the rights are fully taken up. Interim results and other announcements will also have an effect. Thus the price of the shares offered in the new rights issue depends on a great variety of factors, which include:

- the earnings prospects;
- the purpose of the issue;
- the rating of the company's shares;

- the rating of the market sector in which the company operates;
- the general state of the market.

The new market price of the shares of the issuer following the rights issue can be estimated. Broadly, the market capitalisation after the rights issue should be equal to the market capitalisation before the rights issue plus the funds raised by the rights issue. In other words:

(i) status before rights issue:

market capitalisation = old share price × number of shares

(ii) funds raised by the rights issue:

rights price × number of new shares to be issued

=

rights price × number of shares
(after the rights issue − before the rights issue)

(iii) status after the rights issue:

market capitalisation = new share price × number of shares

(iv) since the market capitalisation after the rights issue is equal to the funds raised plus the market capitalisation before the rights issue, then:

new share price × number of shares after rights issue

=

old share price × number of shares before rights issue

+

rights price × (number of shares after the rights issue − number of shares before the rights issue)

or

new share price

=

rights price

+

$$\frac{\text{number of shares before the rights issue}}{\text{number of shares after the rights issue}} \times \text{old share price} - \text{rights price}$$

The new share price will rarely conform exactly to the result given by this calculation because of the influence of the other factors previously mentioned, all of which affect the market's perception of share values.

Bonus shares

Bonus, scrip or capitalisation issues are all one and the same. In this type of issue, the existing shareholders all receive free shares in proportion to the number of shares they already own.

In the absence of complicating factors, such as revised profit forecasts etc, the financial effect of such an issue on the share price is fairly predictable. The market capitalisation of the company cannot be affected by a free issue, since the assets and earnings remain the same while the number of shares simply increases. Hence the effect is to directly dilute the individual share price in proportion to the number of shares issued. For example, a one-for-one scrip would halve the share price.

Bonus issues are usually made for one of two reasons. Firstly, the share price may have become overweight, and it may be felt that the market may "free up" if there are more lower value shares in circulation. Secondly, occasionally, bankers or debenture holders may feel that the level of permanent capital is insufficient to protect their interests. To meet their demands, the company may lock in some of its otherwise distributable reserves by making a scrip issue out of accumulated profit and loss.

2. Finance for private companies

Sooner or later, most successful private companies reach a stage where funds are needed for growth but where there is no desire to incur further borrowing. Under such circumstances, the company can approach either:

- a development capital fund (see Chapter 3) or similar institution with an offer of equity in return for cash; or
- suitable institutions with an offer of preference shares.

In either of these cases, for purposes of the funding proposal, the question of valuing the private company's ordinary or preference shares arises.

Valuing the ordinary shares of a private company

The valuation of a quoted company is easy. It is simply the

market capitalisation, ie the number of shares in issue multiplied by the quoted share price.

However, the shares of private companies are not quoted, and their valuation is much more of an art. Those shares can be valued either on a net assets basis, or on an earnings basis.

The *net assets basis* values the whole company at the net value of its assets less its liabilities. For this purpose, land and buildings have to be revalued, since book figures are likely to be out of date. Such a valuation will probably be of academic interest only to a successful business, since it will probably be earning a very healthy return on those assets and as a result a net assets valuation may well be too low.

The *earnings basis* of valuation reflects the fact that a business is much more than a collection of assets and liabilities. Conceptually, it is an assembly or organism which is capable of producing earnings now and in the future. The value of the business at any point in time is quite simply the value now of that future earnings stream. The value now of that future earnings stream can be assessed by measuring the current earnings using the normal rules of accounting, and by employing a capitalisation factor which reflects earnings potential. In the case of a quoted company, this factor is the Price/Earnings ratio, which was mentioned in the previous Chapter, and which is a prime measure of the market's assessment of the prospects and worth of any quoted company. In other words:

Market capitalisation = Earnings × P/E ratio

Since they are not quoted, private companies cannot have P/E ratios of their own, but there are usually quoted companies of similar business profile, operating characteristics and prospects, and their P/E ratio should be used. Individual company P/Es can be found in the Financial Times, and elsewhere.

Since the shares of a private company are not quoted, and therefore, there is no ready market, a crucial matter in the valuation of an existing shareholding is the question of control. In the case of a new investment made by an institution such as a development capital fund, another important question is that of investor exit.

Thus the valuation of an existing 51% (majority) shareholding in a private company with post-tax earnings of £100,000, operating in a business sector where the average P/E was 15, might be as follows:

$$\text{Market capitalisation} = \text{Earnings} \times \text{P/E ratio}$$
$$= 100,000 \times 15 = 1,500,000$$
$$51\% \text{ shareholding} = .51 \times 1,500,000 = 765,000$$

In addition, it is normal to apply a discount for lack of marketability.

By contrast, the valuation of a 49% shareholding in the same company might be as follows:

$$\text{Market capitalisation (as before)} = 1,500,000$$
$$49\% \text{ shareholding} = .49 \times 1,500,000 \times .7*$$
$$= 514,500$$

The asterisk marks the discount factor applied due to the lack of control, which may range from 10% to 50%. Again, a further discount would be applied for lack of marketability.

Finally, any prospective investor will be looking at two valuations. The first will be the valuation which underlies his purchase, and the second will be the likely future valuation which will help produce his return on investment. The better that future valuation, the lower will be the equity stake which has to be sold in order to provide the needed funds.

Valuing unquoted preference shares

Preference shares usually carry the right to a fixed dividend and no further participation in the profits of the company. For that reason it is the rate of yield and the security of receiving it which are of primary concern to the investor.

Assuming that the preference dividend is well covered by profits, the rate of yield on the preference shares will determine the price of existing preference shares.

For example, a private company has in issue £100,000 nominal of 6% preference shares. Currently, quoted preference shares are yielding 11%. The price of the preference shares will be:

$$100,000 \times \frac{6}{11} = 54,545$$

As with unquoted equity, it is normal to apply a discount for lack of marketability.

Similarly, where the company is seeking to place new unquoted preference shares, the rate which has to be offered needs to relate to the yield offered by quoted preference shares. Those yield rates are normally higher than borrowing rates (reflecting the reduced level of security). However, rates can be reduced if the shares can be made to carry additional rights—for example, participation in profits over a certain level, redemption or conversion.

3. Mergers and acquisitions

At the time of writing, the Stock Exchange has gone through a period of unprecedented activity in the field of mergers and take-overs. The underlying reasons are probably attributable to the high ratings achieved in the market by the predators, which make growth in earnings necessary and acquisition for paper relatively easy.

Acquisitions happen for a great variety of reasons. Synergy is the main motivator where the buyer looks for integration, either vertical to suppliers or customers, or horizontal to complementary products or markets. Other reasons include the desire to dismantle a business and sell off its constituent parts, the need to eliminate competitors, or the need to diversify. In summary, for the acquisition to be successful, the entity created as a result must be demonstrably stronger than either of the entities which existed before.

In all cases where a bid is made on the Stock Exchange, existing shareholders are likely to do well. The predator will inevitably want to make sure that it has full control of its prospective subsidiary. Therefore, it will probably offer the shareholders a price which is better than that at which dealings last took place on the Stock Market.

Each acquisition is different in terms of its business and financial implications. The most straightforward might consist of an agreed valuation paid immediately in cash. The most complex might consist of a share swap (with the vendors receiving shares and debentures issued by the acquiror) with some form of subsequent additional bonus payable if performance targets are reached.

4. Management buy-outs

Over the last few years, perhaps as a consequence of the spate of take-overs, we have seen a good number of successful management buy-outs in the United Kingdom. Some have been very successful indeed, with the management team bringing the company to the Market two to three years after the buy-out.

The essential ingredient of a management buy-out is the existence of a sound business entity which does not fit in with the main business of the owning company, and an attendant experienced management team.

The management buy-out gives the current owners the opportunity to sell out at a better price than break-up value and without incurring redundancy costs or compromising their reputation. The purchasing management are presented with an opportunity to acquire their own stake in their business, albeit at a certain risk to themselves. Last, but not least, the investing institutions are presented with an opportunity to earn a higher return than normal, with risks that are capable of being assessed since both the management and the business are well established.

In bidding for their business, management have no option but to put forward as low a price as possible in the circumstances. Typically, the management team will only be able to put up a fraction of the purchase price, and the rest will have to be provided by a mixture of borrowings and permanent capital. Deferring part of the purchase price is the first consideration. Borrowings should then be maximised within the limits provided by balance sheet security and profit cover. Thereafter, depending on the anticipated level of earnings, preference shares may provide a way of generating capital without sacrificing equity. If possible, equity should be sold only if the sum of borrowings and preference shares cannot provide enough to fund the purchase price.

As with the sale of private company equity to fund development, any prospective investor will be looking at two valuations. The first will be the immediate price which he has to pay for his investment. The second will be the expected value of his investment at the end of some period. The better that future valuation, the lower will be the equity stake which has to be sold in order to provide the needed funds. The investor is often willing to agree to a conditional arrangement in his deal, whereby his share of the equity reduces if the buy-out does well. This sort of arrangement (which is sometimes called a ratchet) can help enhance the position of the management team.

Appendix 1

Statements of Standard Accounting Practice

Accounting practice in the United Kingdom is set out in Statements of Standard Accounting Practice (SSAPs). The contents of the current SSAPs are outlined below:

SSAP 1: Accounting for the results of associated companies

The SSAP defines the way in which significant investments in companies which are not subsidiaries are to be treated in the books of the owning company. In this context significant investments are defined as shareholdings equal to or greater than 20%, and/or ownership situations where the owning company exercises significant influence.

The SSAP envisages that where the above conditions are met, the owning company will include in its consolidated accounts, its share of the results of such companies on an equity accounting basis.

SSAP 2: Disclosure of accounting policies

The SSAP states that it is fundamental to the understanding of financial statements that those who use them should be aware of the main assumptions on which they are based. Accordingly, the accounting policies adopted in preparing the accounts need to be clearly described within those accounts.

The SSAP identifies four fundamental accounting concepts which are always presumed. They are "going concern", "accruals", "consistency" and "prudence".

SSAP 3: Earnings per share

This SSAP deals with the methods of computing earnings per

196

share (EPS), which is an important Stock Market statistic. The SSAP thus applies essentially to listed companies, since private companies do not need to produce EPS data.

The SSAP defines the permissible way of calculating EPS, and requires the basis of calculation to be disclosed and the amount of the EPS to be shown on the face of the profit and loss account.

SSAP 4: The accounting treatment of government grants

This SSAP deals with the accounting treatment of revenue and capital grants available in the United Kingdom.

The SSAP specifies that revenue grants should be matched to the corresponding expenditure. Capital grants should be credited to income over the life of the related fixed assets.

SSAP 5: Accounting for value added tax

This SSAP sets out the treatment of value added tax in items such as sales and cost of sales. VAT is only to be included where it is a cost to the business.

SSAP 6: Extraordinary items and prior period adjustments

This SSAP deals with the accounting treatment of the costs or revenues associated with events which are outside the ordinary activities of the business (defined as extraordinary items), or which arise as a consequence of errors or changes in accounting policy (prior year adjustments).

This SSAP states that adjustments can only be made to prior years if they are material and relate either to the correction of a fundamental error, or are needed to present prior period financial statements fairly for comparative purposes, following a change in accounting policy.

[SSAP 7 has been withdrawn.]

SSAP 8: The treatment of taxation under the imputation system in the accounts of companies

This SSAP describes the approved method of accounting for mainstream corporation tax and advance corporation tax (ACT).

Advance corporation tax is taxation related to the payment of dividends. However, it is substantially offsetable against normal (mainstream) corporation tax.

The SSAP states that any ACT that cannot be offset against mainstream corporation tax should be written off as part of the tax charge. Recoverable ACT may be carried forward as an offset against deferred taxation balances, or alternatively as a deferred asset. Dividends should be shown net of ACT.

SSAP 9: Stocks and work in progress

This SSAP seeks to define the practices which may be used to compute the value of stocks and work-in-progress.

The SSAP defines the stock valuation criterion as the lower of cost or net realisable value. It also defines what is meant by cost and by net realisable value.

SSAP 10: Statements of source and application of funds

This SSAP makes mandatory the inclusion of a statement of source and application of funds within published statutory accounts, and sets out acceptable formats for such statements.

[SSAP 11 has been withdrawn.]

SSAP 12: Accounting for depreciation

This SSAP defines the rules for depreciating fixed assets. It states that all fixed assets with finite useful lives should be depreciated by reference to those lives and to their residual values at the end of those lives (see SSAP 19 for the accounting treatment of investment properties.)

SSAP 13: Accounting for research and development

This SSAP reviews the accounting treatment of research and development expenditure in the light of the potential conflict between the accruals and prudence concepts described in SSAP 2.

The SSAP states that pure and applied research costs are always to be written off immediately they are incurred, and that the same treatment should be adopted for development costs unless there is a clearly defined and potentially viable product.

SSAP 14: Group accounts

This SSAP deals with the presentation of accounts for a group of companies linked through legal ownership.

The SSAP sets out the circumstances under which consolidated accounts need and need not be prepared, requires uniform accounting policies and co-terminous year-end dates to be adopted group wide, and deals with the treatment of acquisitions and disposals.

SSAP 15: Accounting for deferred taxation

The view is widely held that profit after taxation is an important measure of the performance of a business. Consequently, the basis of computing the tax charge is important, particularly since many charges recorded in arriving at book profits are not tax deductible items (for example, book depreciation or general provisions). Conversely, tax depreciation may not be allowable for computation of normal accounting profit. This SSAP defines the extent to which timing differences which arise on the different treatment of items for book and tax purposes need to be reflected in published accounts.

This SSAP states that deferred taxation which is not reasonably expected to reverse in the foreseeable future (3 years at least) need not be provided in the accounts. However, the full amount of such taxation needs to be shown in the notes to accounts.

SSAP 16: Current cost accounting

This SSAP deals with the method of accounting for the effects of specific price inflation. It is not mandatory and is expected to be replaced shortly by a new standard.

SSAP 17: Accounting for post balance sheet events

Events arising after the balance sheet date need to be reflected in the financial statements if they provide additional evidence of conditions that existed at the balance sheet date and materially affect the amounts involved.

Adjusting events, such as post-balance sheet valuations of fixed assets, the result of sales of stocks held at balance sheet date, etc need to be reflected in the balance sheet, since they reduce or clarify uncertainty which existed at the balance sheet date.

Non-adjusting events, such as mergers, acquisitions, issues of shares etc are events which arise after the balance sheet date and concern conditions which did not exist at that time. Consequently, they do not give rise to changes to the financial statements. However, if material, the SSAP requires that they be disclosed.

SSAP 18: Accounting for contingencies

A contingency is a condition which exists at the balance sheet date but of which the outcome will be confirmed only by the occurrence or non-occurrence of certain future events. Examples of such contingencies include lawsuits, insurance claims, political sequestrations and the related compensation etc.

The SSAP states that material losses should be provided for where the probability of the determining event occurring is high. Where the probability of that event occurring is remote, no accrual or disclosure need be made. In the median, where there is a broad degree of uncertainty, disclosure should be made. The accounting and reporting treatment thus depends on probability of outcome.

SSAP 19: Accounting for investment properties

This SSAP states that where fixed assets are held not for consumption within a business but as investments they should not be depreciated, but should be shown in published accounts at open market value.

SSAP 20: Accounting for foreign currency translation

This SSAP sets out the standard accounting practice for foreign currency translation.

The SSAP describes the conditions under which alternative accounting treatments should be used. It envisages that where the interest of the owning company in its subsidiaries is that of an investor (ie the subsidiaries operate as independent units), that interest should be translated using the closing rate ruling at the balance sheet date. However, where the subsidiaries are in essence extensions of the owning company, then their results should be translated on a historical cost basis (called the temporal method).

SSAP 21: Accounting for leases and hire purchase contracts

The effect of a lease is to create a set of rights and obligations related to the use by the lessee of a leased asset for the term of the lease. Those rights are effectively the rewards of ownership, whilst the obligations, including the obligation to pay the rental, effectively constitute the risks of ownership.

The SSAP states that where the rights and risks transferred under a lease are substantially those of outright ownership, barring legal form, the related assets should be recorded in the published accounts as capital assets of the lessee. Thus leases which merely provide finance for the lessee, and other types of leases which meet the criteria set out in the SSAP should be capitalised in the books of the lessee.

SSAP 22: *Accounting for goodwill*

The value of a business as a whole is normally not the same as the value of its individual assets and liabilities. Objective measurement of this difference can usually only be made at the date of acquisition or disposal of the business. However, at that date positive or negative goodwill can arise.

The SSAP states that purchased goodwill should not be carried in the balance sheet of a company or group as a permanent item. It should be written-off, either immediately on acquisition through reserves, or alternatively through the profit and loss account on a systematic basis which reflects its useful life.

SSAP 23: *Accounting for acquisitions and mergers*

This SSAP deals with the accounting treatments which can be used to account for acquisitions and mergers.

The SSAP sets out the conditions under which acquisition accounting has to be used, and those circumstances under which merger accounting can be applied.

Appendix 2

Glossary

This glossary is provided as a guide to the terms used in the financial world. For the sake of completeness, terms in common financial use have been included even when they are not used within this book.

Acceptances: A Bill of Exchange (see below) which has been guaranteed by a bank, and which is therefore eligible to be sold (or discounted) at the finest rates. An acceptance facility is an amount of such guarantees which a bank is prepared to grant to a customer.

Accounting rate of return: The profit available from a project divided by the average capital employed in that project.

Accrual: An estimate of costs incurred in an accounting period where invoices have not yet been received.

Amortisation: the allocation of portions of the cost of an asset to specific periods of time (see also Depreciation).

Asset: A tangible possession or intangible right which is of value to the business.

Auditor: An individual or firm qualified under the Companies Act 1985 to examine the accounts of limited liability companies and certify that they present a true and fair view.

Avoidable costs: Costs which can be turned on or off at the will of management.

Balance sheet: A statement at a point in time of the financial status of a business, showing the composition of the net worth of the business and the capital of the owners.

Bargain: A Stock Exchange transaction.

Bear: An investor who sells shares in anticipation of a fall in the prices.

Bill of Exchange: The precise definition is contained in the Bill of Exchange Act 1882. The definition states that it is an unconditional order in writing, addressed by one person to another, signed by the person giving it, requiring the person to whom it is addressed to pay on demand, or at a fixed or determinable future time, a sum certain in money to, or to the order of, a specified person or to bearer.

Book value: The value of assets as recorded under accounting conventions in the books of account at any point in time.

Breakeven: The level of activity at which contribution is equal to fixed cost.

Bull: An investor who buys shares in anticipation of price increases.

Business Expansion Scheme: Scheme whereby individuals can invest in unquoted companies and deduct the amount of their investment from their taxable income.

Capital: The long term funding available to a business, whether permanently provided by the owners or borrowed for a period of time.

Capital budgeting: Planning the fixed asset and funding needs of a business.

Cash flow: The net cash movement arising from a given business activity over a period of time. It is usually represented by net profit plus depreciation.

Committed costs: Costs which have been incurred and cannot be turned on or off at the will of management.

Companies House: Central public file where each limited liability company is required to file its published accounts and other details of its activities.

Consistency: The accounting convention which requires financial statements to be prepared on the same basis from period to period.

Consolidated accounts: The term used to describe the financial statements produced by a group of companies.

Contribution: The difference between the net value of sales and the related variable costs.

Convertible loan or stock: Borrowings which carry the right to convert into equity capital on predetermined terms.

Corporate planning: The setting of long-term business goals and the formulation of strategy designed to achieve them.

Cost of capital: The outlay required in order to provide the returns required by the providers of capital.

Creditor: One to whom the business owes money.

Debenture: A secured loan set out in a written legal agreement.

Debtor: One who owes the business money.

Deferred tax: That element of taxation which is not immediately payable due to the incidence of tax reliefs and allowances.

Depreciation: A charge to the profit and loss account of a portion of the original or current cost of a long-lived asset, designed to write off that asset over its useful life.

Development capital: Funds specifically designated by the institutions to be invested in established businesses which are planning to expand.

Discounted cash flow: An appraisal technique which takes account of the time value of money.

Dividend: A distribution of profit to shareholders.

Earnings per share: The profit (in pence) attributable to each ordinary share.

Equity: The rights of the owners of a business. In the case of a limited company, the rights of the ordinary shareholders to profit and assets after full provision has been made for the rights of the other providers of capital. See also Shareholders' funds.

Exit: The way in which a venture capitalist realises his investment.

Factoring: The use of debtors as security for borrowings.

FIFO: First-in, first-out cost flow assumption.

Fixed assets: Generally long-lived assets used by the business to provide the infrastructure or capacity to do business.

Fixed costs: Costs which remain constant over a wide range of activity levels.

Floating charge: The preferential right of a lender to realise his loans against the security of unspecified business assets.

Gearing: The total of borrowings as a proportion of the total of capital and reserves.

Going concern: The accounting assumption that the business will continue for the foreseeable future.

Goodwill: The ability of a business to earn profits ahead of its net asset value, normally only quantified in the event of a change of ownership by the purchaser of that business.

Gross profit: Often the same as contribution, but sometimes defined as the difference between the net value of sales and the related variable and fixed costs of production.

Group: A legal structure consisting of a holding company which owns other, subsidiary companies, each being a legal entity in its own right.

Historic cost accounting: The accounting convention which requires assets and liabilities to be recorded broadly at their original cost.

Holding company: The top company in a group.

Hurdle rate: The minimum internal rate of return required of a project to make it acceptable for investment purposes.

Incremental cost: The isolated extra costs associated with a specific course of action.

Internal rate of return: The discount rate that makes the net present value of a project equal to zero.

Introduction: A way of obtaining a quotation without the need for extensive marketing. It presupposes that the shares are already widely held.

Issuing house: An institution which advises companies seeking to raise capital on the Stock Exchange.

Leasing: Strictly the right to the use of specific fixed assets for a stated period in return for a rent. However, in the past also largely used as a means of separating ownership and use of assets.

LIBOR: Stands for London inter-bank offer rate. It is the rate at which deposits are offered on the inter-bank market. This rate is constantly changing.

LIFO: Last-in, first-out cost flow assumption.

Limiting factor: An operating or financial constraint which restricts business performance.

Liquidity: The extent to which a business has ready cash, near cash, and borrowing facilities available.

Loan covenant: Specific financial conditions, such as balance sheet ratios, with which a company has agreed to comply as part of its terms of borrowing.

Management buy-out: The acquisition of part of a business by the managers of that business.

Marginal costing: An approach to financial decision-making which is based on an analysis of costs into fixed and variable elements and an assessment of the incremental costs associated with any contemplated course of action.

Market capitalisation: The value at which the company stands as perceived by the Stock Exchange. That value equals the share price multiplied by the number of shares in issue.

Materiality: The concept that changes and amendments which do not affect the users' perception of the position shown in a set of published accounts need not be included therein.

Merchant bank: A specialist bank that does not handle customer current account business, but which deals with the financing of special situations and the provision of advice on corporate financial matters.

Minority shareholders: The owners of that (small) part of a company's share capital which is not held by a majority shareholder.

Money markets: A grouping of commercial and merchant banks that provide short-term finance from funds deposited with them.

Negative pledge: An undertaking given by a borrower normally in connection with a term loan, that he will not give the assets of the business as security for any other borrowings.

Net present value: The net value now of cash flows which are due to take place in the future.

Net profit: Profit after all costs including interest but excluding taxation and dividends.

Net worth: The total of fixed assets and working capital less long term liabilities. Otherwise, the amount of share capital and reserves.

Offer for sale: An offer by an issuing house of securities at a stated price direct to the public.

Ordinary shares: The class of capital which owns the business. It entitles the holders to all net profits remaining after other providers of capital have been paid. It is also entitled to repayment of capital and all of the surplus on winding up, but only after all the other providers of funds have been repaid.

Over-the-counter market: An arrangement under which securities of companies not listed on the Stock Exchange are traded by certain investment organisations, who either act as principals and take the securities onto their book or who match buyers and sellers.

Payback period: The period of time it will take for a project to generate sufficient cash to pay for itself.

Placing: An offer of shares or loan capital to a limited range of investors.

PLC: Public limited company.

Preference shares: A class of capital which entitles the holders to a rate of dividend ahead of the ordinary shareholders, and on liquidation, to receive repayment of their capital before the ordinary shareholders. Rights to accumulate, redeem, or participate may also be attached to preference shares.

Prepayments: Payments made for goods and services the benefits of which will be received in the future.

Present value: The value now of a future cash transaction.

Price/earnings ratio: The price of one ordinary share divided by its attributable earnings (ie the earnings per share).

Profit and loss account: A summary of the income and expenditure of a given entity for a given period of time.

Provision: An amount put aside to cover losses, as for example a bad debt provision or a stock obsolescence provision.

Prudence: The accounting convention which disregards profits unless they are certain, but books losses when they can be foreseen.

Published accounts: Annual accounts required by law of all limited liability companies.

Ratchet: Arrangement, usually in a management buy-out or similar situation, by which management can increase their share of a business in the event that forecasts are achieved.

Reserves: Amounts retained from the business, either from profits or from capital transactions.

Responsibility accounting: A method of allocating functional responsibility and authority for execution of budgets to the appropriate individuals within the organisation.

Rights issue: An invitation to existing shareholders to subscribe for further shares in proportion to their existing shareholdings.

Scrip issue: A free issue of shares to existing shareholders in proportion to their shareholdings.

Seed capital: The initial capital required to start up a business.

Sensitivity analysis: An analysis of the effect on financial forecasts of variation of key assumptions.

Shareholders' funds: The total of paid up share capital and reserves.

Simulation: Prediction of the effect on the business of different economic conditions or operating constraints.

Source and application of funds statement: A financial statement showing for a period the sources of funds and the amounts, and the ways in which those funds were used.

SSAP: Statement of standard accounting practice, issued by the accounting institutes.

Stag: An investor who applies for a new issue solely with the object of making an immediate profit in anticipation of the initial Stock Exchange dealing price being higher than the issue price.

Statutory accounts: See Published accounts.

Stock Exchange: An established market which matches the capital needs of managers with the return requirements of investors.

Sunk costs: Costs which have already been incurred and cannot be avoided, which are therefore irrelevant to decisions about the future.

Tender offer: An offer by an issuing house of securities at a minimum subscription price direct to the public.

Underwriting: A guarantee given by a third party that it will subscribe for any securities not taken up in the normal course of a new issue.

USM: A capital market established for the smaller company that seeks a market for its shares and the ability to raise funds.

Value added: The net income stream created by the business for payment of internal costs, including employees, providers of borrowed capital, taxation and owners of the business.

Variable costs: Costs which vary in proportion to the level of activity.

Variance: Difference between expected and actual results.

Venture capital: Funds specifically designated by the institutions to be invested in businesses which are not necessarily established, but which have strong future prospects.

Winding up: Liquidation of the operations of a company, distribution of its assets, and ultimately dissolution of the legal entity concerned.

Working capital: The continually fluctuating business assets, net of liabilities, which are used in the day-to-day trading of the business.

Zero-based budgeting: The build up of budgets from basic information about the physical activities of the business (rather than with reference to the financial performances of previous periods).

Index

page

Acceptance credits. 47-48
Accounting conventions. 176-181
Accounts — see *Financial accounts, Management accounts*
Accruals. 32, 33
Acquisition 193-194
Amortisation. 37-39
Asset(s):
    capital. 108-134
    current. 35
    fixed. 35, 37-39, 177-178, 183
    turnover 149-150
    value of. 31-32
Audit 12, 167-168, 169, 173, 174-175
Averaging 148

Balance sheet 27-29, 35-36, 175
Block discounting. 48-49
Bonus issues 190
Book-keeping, principles of 24-32
Borrowing(s) 41, 42, 45-51, 59-60, 160
Break-up value 31, 194
Breakeven. 69-88
    calculation of 70-75
    pricing and 76-88
Budgeting: 8-9
    control 140-146
    zero-based. 142-143
    see also *Corporate planning; Forecasting; Strategic planning*
Business expansion scheme. 53-54
Business plan 155-158, 164-165

Capacity. 6-7, 8, 83, 85-86
Capital 40-60
    assets 108-134
    borrowing. 41, 42, 45-51, 59, 160
    budgeting 109-110
    cost of 40-41, 58-60
    equity 42, 52, 160, 161-162
    expenditure 108-134

  permanent 51-57
  raising 42, 45-51, 53-57, 154-165, 188-193
  return on 6, 32-33, 40, 42-45, 58-60, 76, 112-114
                                            123-125, 148-149
  risk 42-45, 51-52, 58
  venture 54, 162-163
  working 36, 89-107, 161
Capitalisation issue 190
Cash 180
  collection of 19-21
  flow:
    capital expenditure and 111-112
    discounted 118-125
    effect of accounting conventions on 36-37
    forecast 155-158
  payback, and 114-115
  role of 15-17
Comparison of performance-see *Performance analysis*
Contribution 67-69, 70
Control:
  business of 4-11, 13-14
  performance, of 135-153
Corporate:
  finance 187-195
  objectives 135-136
  planning 4-11, 135-153
Costs:
  analysis of 65-67
  assessment of future 5-6
  credit, of 103-105
  direct-see *variable*
  fixed 5-6, 19, 63, 70, 75, 77, 85-88, 142-143
  indirect-see *fixed*
  nature of 62-67
  production 18-19, 76-78
  semi-variable 64
  "step" 64
  structure 65-67
  variable 5-6, 19, 62-63, 68, 75, 77
Credit:
  costs of 103-105
  effect of on cash flow 16, 93
  management of 102-107
  sale, on 25-26
Creditors, management of 106-107
Cumulative preference share 52

Debenture 50-51
Debtors 102-107, 179-180

Deferred ordinary share 52
Depreciation 37-39, 177
Development capital 54-55
Directors' report 174
Discounted cash flow 118-125
Discounts 19-21, 104, 105, 106
Dividend yield 186
Double entry book-keeping 27-30

Earnings basis of valuation 191
Economic trends 7
Equity 42, 52, 160, 161-162
Evaluation of capital projects 109, 110-125
Expansion 8, 79, 128
    see also *Capital expenditure*
Expenses 33

Factoring 48
Finance, raising 42, 45-51, 53-57, 154-165, 188-193
Financial accounts 1-3, 166-186
    audit of 12, 167-168, 169, 173, 174-175
    purpose of 167-172
    statutory requirements 11-12, 167, 172-173
    "true and fair view" 169-170
Fixed assets 35, 37-39, 177-178, 183
Flotation as means of raising capital 55-57
Forecasting 155-158, 164-165
Funding 42, 45-51, 53-57, 154-165, 188-193
Funds, source and application of 176

Gearing 44-46, 185
Glossary 202-209
"Going concern" 31-32, 176-177
Gross profit 34

Industry trends 7
Inflation allowance 148
Information, financial 1-21
    purpose of 3-11
    quality of 10-11
    selection of 17-21
    users of 11-14
    see also *Financial accounts*
Insurance company as source of capital 55
Interest cover 45, 185
Inventory-see *Stock*
Investment-see *Capital expenditure*
Invoice discounting 48-49

Land and buildings-see *Capital expenditure; Fixed assets*

Leasing 49-50, 110
Liabilities:
   current 35, 180-181
   long term 35, 181
   value of 31-32
Limited company 23-24, 166
Loss, correct calculation of 8

Management accounts 1-3, 12-14, 144-15
Management buy-outs 194-195
Merger and acquisition 193-194
Mortgages 46-47

Net assets basis of valuation 191
Net profit 34

Off-balance sheet borrowing 50
Operating:
   ratios 146-153
   skills and constraints 6-7, 8
Ordinary share 52
"Over the counter" market 57
Overdrafts 46
"Overtrading" 17, 94

Partnership 23
Payback period, as method of evaluating capital
   projects 114-118
Pension fund as source of capital 55
Performance analysis 135-153, 182
Planning, corporate 4-11, 135-153
Planning, strategic 7, 136-139
Plant-see *Capital expenditure; Fixed assets*
Preference share 52, 192-193
Price/earnings ratio 185, 191
Pricing 76-88
Probability 128-131
Product design 18
Production:
   capacity 83, 85-86
   costs 18-19
Profit
   and loss account 37, 175
   calculation of 32-34
   capital projects and 113-114, 123
   centre 22, 144
   gross 34
     see also *Contribution*
   meaning of 14-15

net 34
pricing for 76, 78-88
Prudence 32

Ratio analysis 146-153, 181-186
Raw materials-see *Stock; Working capital assets*
Reporting of business results 9-11, 144-153
Responsibility, allocation of 140, 143-144
Return on capital invested 6, 32-33, 40, 42-45, 58-60, 76,
                                    112-114, 123-125, 148-149
Revenue 33
maximising 142
Rights issue 188-189
Risk, impact of 125-134
"Romalpa" clauses........................... 25-26, 27, 104

Sale and leaseback 47
Sale, time of 25-26
Sales, return on 149, 150-151
Scrip issue 190
Sensitivity analysis.............................. 131
Share(s):
types of 52
valuation of 190-193
Sole trader 23
Standard accounting practice.................. 31-32, 170-171
Standard deviation............................. 130-131
Statements of Standard Accounting Practice 31, 171, 181,
                                              196-201
Statutory accounts-see *Financial accounts*
Stock:
costs of 96-98
funding of....................................... 92-93
level of 19, 90, 96-102
turn... 98-99
value of 30-31, 178-179
Stock Exchange 55-57, 187-190
Strategic planning 7, 136-139
"SWOT" analysis................................ 137-139

Take-over 193-194
Title, retention of.......................... 25-26, 27, 104
Transactions:
recording of 24-30
value of.. 30-31
"True and fair view" 169-170, 176

Uncertainty, impact of.......................... 125-134
Unlisted Securities Market 57

Valuation of shares 190-193
Value added 67-69
Value, transaction, of............................... 30-31
Venture capital 54, 162-163
Volume target 71-75, 80-81

Work in progress-see *Stock; Working capital assets*
Working capital 36, 89-107
    assets................................ 89-91, 108-109, 161
    debtors and 102-107
    stocks and 96-102
    time-lags, effect of, on 91-93
    volume effects on 93-96